Successful Portrait Painting

Successful Portrait Painting

By
JOHN HOWARD SANDEN
with Elizabeth R. Sanden

WATSON-GUPTILL PUBLICATIONS/NEW YORK

SENATOR ROBERT C. BYRD (frontispiece)
Oil on canvas, 40 x 28" (101 x 71 cm). This is a preliminary study I
painted in Senator Byrd's office in the Capitol. The full-length por-
trait, measuring 84 x 42" (213 x 107 cm), is being executed as this
book goes into production.

First published 1981 in the United States and Canada by Watson-Guptill Publications,
a division of Billboard Publications, Inc.,
1515 Broadway, New York, N.Y. 10036

Library of Congress Cataloging in Publication Data
Sanden, John Howard.
   Successful portrait painting.
   Bibliography: p.
   Includes index.
   1. Portrait painting.   I. Sanden, Elizabeth R.
II. Title.
ND1300.S2 1981   751.45'42   81-7455
ISBN 0-8230-5003-3   AACR2

Manufactured in Japan

First Printing, 1981

Edited by Bonnie Silverstein
Designed by Jay Anning
Set in 11-point Palatino

TO DR. BRYANT M. KIRKLAND

who, through his creative ministry
and generous spirit,
is teaching us
that true success comes
through faith, love, obedience, and service
. . . even in New York.

We would like to express our appreciation

. . . to Don Holden, for his friendship over many years,
his wise counsel and professional expertise.

. . . to Bonnie Silverstein, our editor, for her enthusiastic,
judicious, and highly creative shaping of the manu-
script.

. . . to Andrea Ericson, for her unfailing kindness and
wise guidance.

. . . to Jay Anning, for the attractive design of this book.

. . . to Tony Mysak, who made the copies of all the paintings with care and sensitivity.

. . . to Dan Demetriad, for his great help with a multitude
of photographic matters.

. . . to our daughter Pamela for being wonderful, sweet,
and patient.

Contents

MOLLY BROWN AND MUFFIN, by Elizabeth R. Sanden
Oil on canvas, 30 x 24" (76 x 61 cm), collection Mr. and Mrs. Richard Ballantine.

Foreword

I will never forget the first time I saw John Howard Sanden at work on a professional portrait commission. I had seen him demonstrate his wonderful talent for capturing a likeness of the model in a head study demonstration executed before a large audience. In a most dramatic and interesting fashion, John Sanden can attack a plain canvas and paint *premier coup* (alla prima) a startling likeness in about two hours. He paints in an orderly, step-by-step procedure, which is fully described in his first book, *Painting the Head in Oil* (Watson-Guptill, 1976).

My first introduction to the professional portrait commission, however, seemed to contradict everything I had seen Sanden do. The enormous amount of preplanning and preliminary work involved before even coming near oil colors seemed unbelievable to me.

I have now come to realize, after many hours of discussion on the subject and actual practice at executing portraits myself, that all of these steps, to be described in the pages of this book, *are necessary* in order to paint a portrait *premier coup*—freshly, directly, and with assurance, so that the strokes being painted are as close to the final passages of paint as possible.

John Sanden spends weeks, even months, preparing the research material he needs to execute a professional portrait commission, including meetings with the subject, photographs, a head study, a compositional study, and an accurate drawing. But when he does step to the canvas, brush in hand, he paints directly and with assurance for several days straight, in order to execute the painting premier coup—wet paint into wet paint—working from the first toward a finished painting.

As I began to learn Sanden's methods, I soon began to understand that these preliminary steps are absolutely essential to the success of the portrait. I also began to realize that there is no substitute for painting a subject from life and that an artist who paints from photographs alone will never be as successful as one who combines photography and other reference material with one or more sittings with the subject. I therefore encouraged him to teach his technique and procedures to advanced students.

This book, *Successful Portrait Painting*, is intended for experienced artists who want to perfect their skills in the art of portraiture. It describes the logical, organized procedure used by John Howard Sanden in executing a professional portrait commission. There are obviously many ways to execute a successful portrait, but John Howard Sanden has found that the method described in this book works for him, and he is willing to share it with others.

Elizabeth R. Sanden
New York, 1981

Introduction

In the introduction to my first book, *Painting the Head in Oil*, I described portrait painting as the "Mount Everest" of painting. And so it is. If man is the highest form of creation, then the recreation of man in a painting is the highest and most challenging form of painting. A visit to any of the great museums reinforces at once the conviction that portraiture has always presented the greatest challenges to the masters of painting.

I am genuinely thrilled by the enthusiasm of young people today for the art of portrait painting. It has an intense fascination for talented and ambitious young painters. They crowd our big annual seminar here in New York each summer (for information about the National Portrait Seminar, write to National Art Seminars Corporation, Washington, Conn. 06794.), and they jam the studios of The Art Students League to bursting. So the appeal of portraiture remains strong. These young people sense in it—rightly—an avenue for the rich expression of their creativity, plus the opportunity for financial reward for which it is famous.

This book is the result of years of practical experience in the field of portrait painting. In these pages I will show you examples of my own work and tell you how I went about creating them. I also will describe my methods in detail and try to give you my reasons for doing what I did. Of course I do not expect you to agree with everything I say, nor do I expect you to adopt all of my procedures. I only expect that you will do as I have done: study the work of a number of artists you admire, and adopt that portion of their methods that is sympathetic to your own desires.

You will not discover very many "shortcuts" in this book. Every artist who has made portrait painting his profession has discovered soon enough that success is based on much work. Portraiture is a demanding and exacting profession, and those who have mastered it have done so through a combination of intense desire and a willingness to work unrelentingly. Since drawing and painting are so intertwined in portraiture, several years of good old-fashioned academic drawing under a disciplined, critical, and skilled master are absolutely essential, followed by—or concurrent with—an equal amount of painting from the live model.

It is assumed that anyone entering the field of portraiture has had a thorough training in the arts of drawing and painting, since these two disciplines intertwine so completely in portraiture. Several years of rigorous exercise in good old-fashioned academic drawing under a disciplined, critical, and skilled master are absolutely essential, followed by—or concurrent with—an equal amount of painting from the live model.

My own progress into portrait painting was natural and sequential. I was interested in drawing and painting from my earliest childhood—in fact, to the exclusion of almost everything else. When I was nine years old, my father (a Presbyterian clergyman) gave me my first "lessons" in art. He set before me a copy of *Abraham Lincoln: His Life in Pictures* by Stefan Lorant, a stack of white typewriter paper, and a fountain pen with blue ink, and he instructed me to copy, one by one, every picture in the book. I rendered every hair on Lincoln's head and every mole and crease in his fascinating face. This was followed by copying from *The Life of Christ Visualized* and many more books.

When I was old enough to enter the Minneapolis School of Art, I was fortunate to get in on the final years of a truly great instructor: Gustav Krollmann of Vienna, who taught figure drawing in a marvelously academic, "old-fashioned" way. He taught *constructive* drawing, where the forms were built on a closely observed structure of angular measurements. He was deliberate and methodical. His lectures on the Italian Renaissance were thrilling and inspirational.

My interests were in the field of illustration, and I moved naturally into this work after graduation from art school. For a number of years I specialized in work for religious publications, before evolving into "human interest" subjects for calendar publishers and others. Always, the human face and figure were the central themes of my work.

In 1967 I received an assignment from the *Reader's Digest* to illustrate a novel that had a religious theme. This was a momentous event for me, because it was to lead me into portraiture as a separate and specific field. I began to paint many portraits for the *Digest*, and this work brought me frequently to New York. I knew that there was much still to learn—and that New York was the place to learn it. So I made the decisive move in 1969. Leaving a lifetime of associations in the Midwest, I came to New York to live and enrolled part-time in The Art Students League under Samuel Edmund Oppenheim. Mr. Oppenheim is one of America's most distinguished painters of portraits. The two years during which I was associated with him were absolutely invaluable. He was dignified, courtly, soft-spoken, elegant, warm—and a master painter. I had an intense desire to be like him. When Mr. Oppenheim retired from teaching, I was appointed to lead his class at The Art Students League, and I began to receive portrait assignments from Portraits, Incorporated, the famous gallery that has represented so many leading artists over the years. I am happy to say that both associations have continued without interruption to the present day.

This book will tell you everything that I have learned over these years. The most important lessons, of course, I cannot teach. They are the lessons of self-discipline, determination, artistic dissatisfaction, and enthusiasm that make up the life of a growing artist. In your career as an artist, it is growth that really matters. Achievement is hollow if it is not followed by a finer achievement. Every painting that you do must be better than the one that preceded it.

Please read through this book with a view to selecting those ideas and methods that will be helpful to you. Freely discard those that are not compatible with your instincts. By this process of selection and elimination, you will arrive at your own methods and style.

There is no way I can adequately acknowledge the enormous contribution to this book made by my lovely wife Elizabeth. She has worked intimately, selflessly, and tirelessly at my side throughout the past eight years, assisting in thousands of ways as the paintings in this book were made. Her own outstanding talents as a painter—she has done many fine portraits—have helped immeasurably in her roles as counselor and helpful critic. In the production of this book itself, she has worked painstakingly and imaginatively, and I am deeply grateful. Elizabeth joins me in wishing you every success in the fascinating world of portrait painting.

John Howard Sanden
New York, 1981

SAMUEL EDMUND OPPENHEIM
One of the most distinguished names in the history of American portrait painting, Samuel Oppenheim is also a great teacher of painting. He was my instructor at the Art Students League of New York, where his demonstrations of portrait technique were dazzling, virtuoso performances. He also paints a host of appealing subjects in a soft, sensuous style of "romantic realism." Today he divides his time between his studios in Florida and Cape Cod. (Photo by Peter Juley, New York.)

Part I
The Portrait Studio

1

Painting Equipment and Materials

2. NEW YORK STUDIO
My artistic life centers about this studio. It is conveniently located in the heart of mid-Manhattan.

My studios, both in Connecticut (Figure 1) and New York (Figure 2) contain equipment and materials I find essential and convenient for painting portraits. Describing my studio equipment should give you ideas for equipping and arranging your own studio.

STUDIO LIGHTING
The north window will always remain important since it allows the artist to see his work by natural light without the disturbance of direct sunlight. Recently, a number of companies (thank goodness) have developed excellent fluorescent units that come very close to duplicating natural light on the Kelvin scale. I use Criticolor bulbs (manufactured by the Verd-A-Ray Corporation, headquartered in Toledo, Ohio) in both my New York and Connecticut studios. These lights enable me to work well into the evening hours and on gray, rainy days. I pity the artists of old who had to depend on Mother Nature for ideal painting conditions!

EASELS
You will need at least two easels, one for studio work and a portable one for on-location travel. I have three types: a studio easel (Figure 3), a radial easel (Figure 4), and a French easel (Figure 5).

MODEL STAND
The amazing model stand pictured in Figure 6 was designed and built for me by my artist friends and colleagues Robert Bruce Williams and Steven Moppert. After many years of discussing the problem of painting on location without a portable model stand, they came up with this solution and presented it to me at the 1980 National Portrait Seminar in New York. The completely collapsible stand is made of sturdy aluminum and breaks down to fit into the leather case shown next to it. The holes are there to lighten the total weight, which is fifty pounds. The platform is hinged to fold into the case, and the steps fold up like a Chinese puzzle. I was thrilled at receiving this wonderful, lavish gift, and I promptly threw out my studio model stand, which took up a great deal of space. Now I can set up and take down my stand as I wish.

BACKGROUND SCREENS
I own two screens: one for studio work, and a lighter portable model for travel (Figure 7).

1. COUNTRY STUDIO (page 14)
My studio in Connecticut provides a tranquil contrast to the bustling city. Outside that window, the Shepaug River sparkles in the sunshine.

3. STUDIO EASEL (above)
This is the easel in my Connecticut studio, where I have a 16-foot (4.9 m) ceiling. One disadvantage of this easel is that if you don't have high ceilings, it's impossible to raise the easel in order to work on the lower part of a large canvas. This is a very old easel given to me by close friend Basil Baylin, and I don't know the brand name or if it's still being made. The Anco Greenwich easel, however, can be used in rooms of conventional height, and is the one I use in New York.

5. FRENCH EASEL (above)
This is an excellent easel for travel, since it folds down to paintbox size and can hold your oil colors and brushes. I always use this easel when I travel by airplane to work on location.

4. RADIAL EASEL (left)
This easel folds down to a cumbersome but manageable size for travel. It is sturdy and can hold a framed painting securely. I have taken this easel on visits to client's homes for unveiling the finished work and last-minute corrections, as well as to on-location painting trips.

6. MODEL STAND
A model stand is useful in seeing the sitter in the right perspective. I used to own a wooden platform, but discarded it after receiving this sturdy, collapsible stand as a gift.

7. BACKGROUND SCREEN
This background screen consists of two tripods and a horizontal bar. About a yard of fabric is draped over the bar and pinned at either side by two paper clips. It is sturdy, but not really portable. Therefore, for travel, I use a much smaller, homemade apparatus (which you see on the floor). It consists of two lightweight folding tripods and three sections of curtain rod.

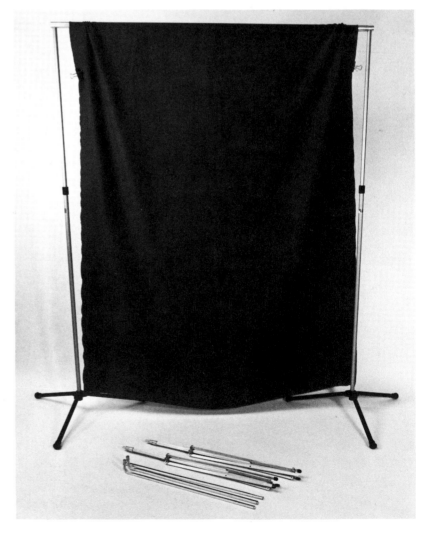

MIRROR

A mirror mounted in such a way that a quick glance over your shoulder shows you a new perspective on your work is an excellent aid to self-criticism (Figure 8). Seeing the image in reverse can help you to spot errors or weak passages.

STORAGE CABINETS AND CHESTS

To keep my studios neat and organized, I store my materials and projects in an old dental chest and record cabinet I found while antique-hunting (Figure 9) and in a twenty-drawer chest and compartmental cabinet (Figure 10). I also keep a taboret near my easel for easy access to a number of supplies I use while painting (Figure 11).

PALETTE AND STAND

My palette is a 30 x 36" (76 x 91 cm) sheet of glass placed over a white board. It rests on a wooden stand with a cast-iron drawing-board tripod as its base. Its two drawers hold my tubed oil colors, arranged in labeled sequence so they can be located quickly when needed (Figure 12).

8. MIRROR
The mirror in my Connecticut studio is mounted on an antique display easel I found in a junk shop.

9. DENTAL CHEST AND RECORD CABINET
I store paints, brushes, mediums, and varnishes in the various-sized drawers of this dental chest, and keep photographs and sketches in the record cabinet beside it. The cabinet is on a tray with casters so I can move it easily.

10. STORAGE CABINET

This twenty-drawer chest, with additional compartments below, helps keep the studio organized. Each assignment and project has its own labeled drawer for photographs, sketches, and miscellaneous items related to that job. Larger items may be kept in the storage compartments below. When a painting is completed and leaves the studio, the drawer is cleaned out and the space made ready for a new job. I designed this cabinet and had it built for me by a carpenter.

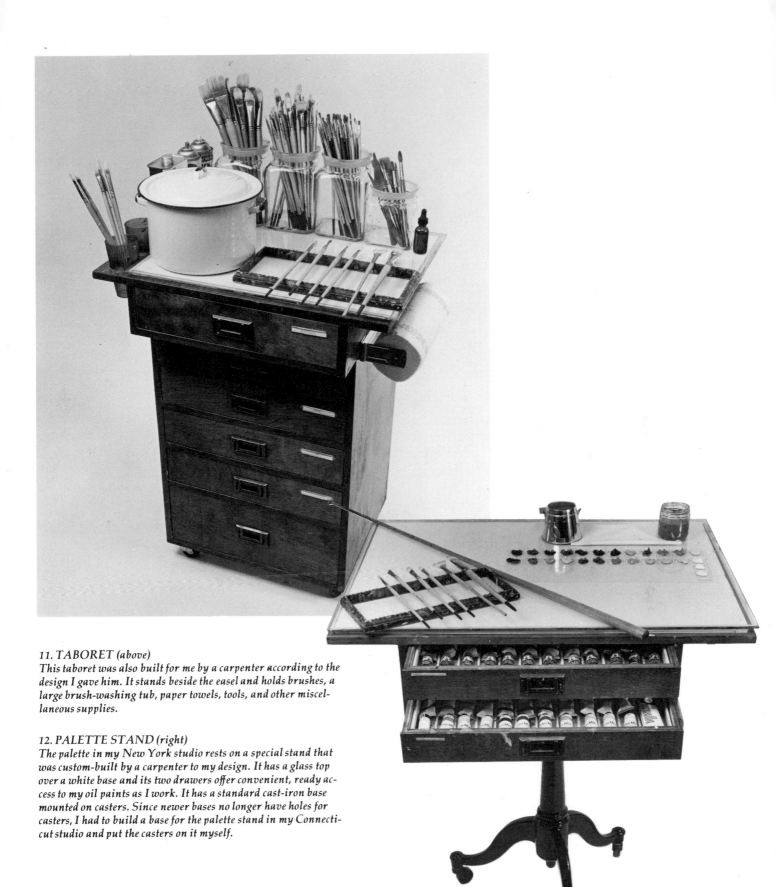

11. TABORET (above)
This taboret was also built for me by a carpenter according to the design I gave him. It stands beside the easel and holds brushes, a large brush-washing tub, paper towels, tools, and other miscellaneous supplies.

12. PALETTE STAND (right)
The palette in my New York studio rests on a special stand that was custom-built by a carpenter to my design. It has a glass top over a white base and its two drawers offer convenient, ready access to my oil paints as I work. It has a standard cast-iron base mounted on casters. Since newer bases no longer have holes for casters, I had to build a base for the palette stand in my Connecticut studio and put the casters on it myself.

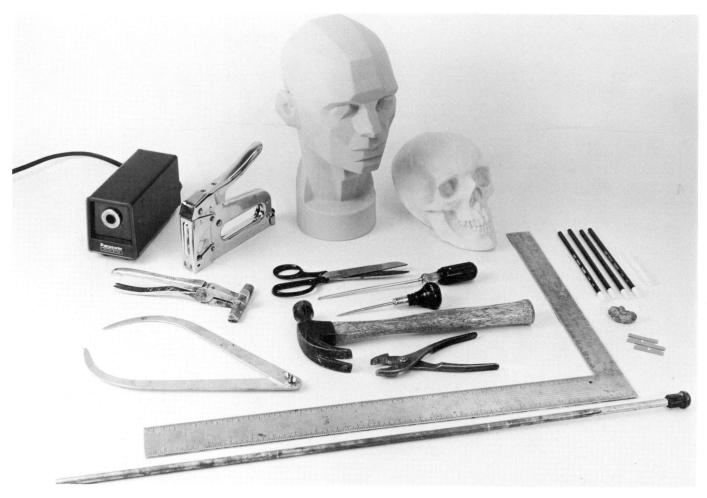

In addition to the equipment I've listed, I use a number of assorted supplies and materials (Figures 13 and 14). A more detailed description of the items follows.

CANVAS
Although not pictured in the photographs, I recommend Kent no. 125 SP (single-primed) canvas, made by Frederix, for portrait work. It has a uniform, moderately smooth surface and is single primed with an oil-based primer.

MEDIUMS AND VARNISHES
Most of the mediums and varnishes I use are shown in Figure 14. They include:

Taubes Copal Painting Medium, Light. I use this sparingly to thin paint if necessary.

Weber Sphinx Retouch Varnish. This varnish may be brushed over a dry painting before releasing it to clients. It can also be used to bring up colors on a dry painting when retouching certain areas.

Winsor & Newton Damar Varnish. This final varnish should be applied about a year after the painting is completed. I usually don't get the opportunity to apply this coat since the portraits leave the studio on completion. I recommend that my clients contact someone to apply this final varnish.

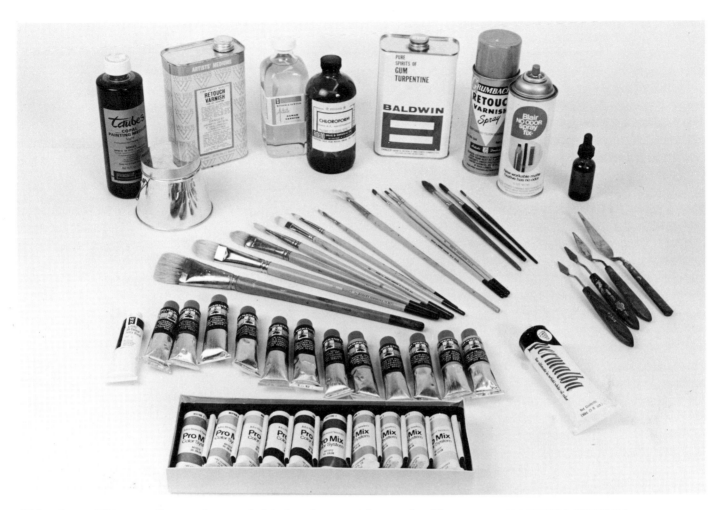

Chloroform. This excellent solvent of dried paint must be used with extreme care in a well-ventilated room. It is capable of loosening dry paint and removing it completely down to the canvas so a new premier coup approach can be made. It is available from pharmacies.

Turpentine. I use pure gum spirits of turpentine to thin paint for a loose, washy effect. I also use it to remove most of the paint from my brushes before scrubbing them with soap and water to complete the cleaning process.

Grumbacher Retouch Varnish in Spray Can. This varnish may be sprayed on a dry painting before retouching dry areas of the portrait. It makes the paint appear wet and shiny and is easier to use than brush-on varnish.

Blair "No Odor" Spray Fix. This may be used over a pencil or charcoal drawing to keep it from smudging when you begin to paint.

Oil of Cloves. This product, available at a pharmacy, may be used to keep oil colors from drying for several days. It should be used sparingly—one drop added and mixed into each large mound of paint.

Brush Washer. This standard brush washer is available from most art material dealers. I also have a large tub holding a can of turpentine for final cleaning prior to washing in soap and water.

14. PAINTING SUPPLIES
Here are the painting supply items I use. You will find a brief description of each in the text of this chapter. They are: (A) Taubes copal painting medium, light (the medium comes in light and heavy—that is, thin and thick—viscosities), (B) Weber Sphinx retouch varnish, (C) Winsor & Newton damar varnish, (D) chloroform, (E) turpentine, (F) Grumbacher retouch varnish (spray can), (G) Blair "No Odor" spray fixative, (H) oil of cloves (eyedropper bottle), (I) brush washer, (J) brushes, (K) standard oil colors, (L) premixed portrait colors, (M) Permalba white, (N) painting and palette knives.

BRUSHES

The brushes I use are also pictured in Figure 14. Here is a description and the number of each that I recommend you have on hand.

Bristle Broads. Robert Simmons Series 40 "Signet," no. 18. These large brushes are used mainly for broad background passages. I recommend having four of these.

Bristle Filberts. Robert Simmons Series 42 "Signet," nos. 12, 10, 8, 6, 4 and 2. These are the brushes I use the most. I find they give me the most control over the stroke without allowing me to become too fussy. Ideally you should have six of each size.

Bristle Fan Blenders. Robert Simmons Series 48, nos. 6 and 2 (no. 2 is not shown). These brushes should not be overused, but they are good for softening edges here and there. Try to have at least two of each size.

Sable Long Flats. Robert Simmons Series 68L, nos. 6, 4, and 2. These brushes are used for fine details that can't be achieved with the bristle brushes. I recommend that you have four of each size.

Red Sable Rounds. Robert Simmons Series 65R, nos. 12, 9, and 7. I use these brushes for blending small passages in the face and for placing small highlights. You should have two or more of each size.

STANDARD OIL COLORS

I use Rembrandt or Winsor & Newton colors for most of my portrait work, although I suspect that the less expensive colors are just as good. The chart in Figure 15 shows their arrangement on my palette.

EARTH COLORS

Burnt Umber. This is an essential basic brown color. It is semi-opaque and one of the fastest drying colors on the palette.

Yellow Ochre. This is a basic flesh tone and is used in almost every mixture for light and halftone areas.

Venetian Red. This is a beautiful, strong, opaque color with very strong tinting power. It is an excellent addition to ruddy flesh tones.

Burnt Sienna. This semitransparent reddish brown color is used in almost all shadow areas.

CADMIUMS AND ALIZARIN

Cadmium Yellow Light. There are many beautiful yellows, but my personal choice is cadmium yellow light, which is opaque, clean, and extremely brilliant. Used sparingly in painting flesh, it may be mixed with alizarin crimson and white for a beautiful cool highlight.

Cadmium Red Light. This is my favorite color on the palette, and it is the only one of the cadmium reds that will do the job. It is beautiful, opaque, intense, high key, and clean. You cannot paint portraits without it!

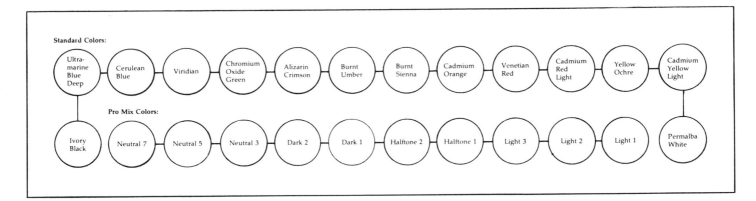

Standard Colors:

Ultra-marine Blue Deep — Cerulean Blue — Viridian — Chromium Oxide Green — Alizarin Crimson — Burnt Umber — Burnt Sienna — Cadmium Orange — Venetian Red — Cadmium Red Light — Yellow Ochre — Cadmium Yellow Light

Pro Mix Colors:

Ivory Black — Neutral 7 — Neutral 5 — Neutral 3 — Dark 2 — Dark 1 — Halftone 2 — Halftone 1 — Light 3 — Light 2 — Light 1 — Permalba White

Cadmium Orange. The third cadmium color on my palette is another intense, opaque color with powerful tinting strength. Cadmium orange is particularly good for warming up shadow areas that have gone too dark or dead looking.

Alizarin Crimson. This is a color I have trouble categorizing. It is a transparent red and I love it on the portrait palette. It is cool and, when added to white, makes a delicious pink color.

COOL COLORS
Viridian. This is a beautiful, transparent green that I don't think I could do without. I use it in shadow mixtures.

Chromium Oxide Green. This green is used a a foil for viridian in that it is intense and opaque. I could probably get along without it, but it makes for interesting variation in the shadows.

Ultramarine Blue. A traditional blue in the history of oil painting, ultramarine blue is partially opaque and has strong tinting power.

Cerulean Blue. I use cerulean blue as a foil for ultramarine. It's opaque, but lighter in tinting strength than ultramarine and is rather a warm blue when white is added.

NEUTRALS
Ivory Black. I complete my palette with ivory black on one side and white on the other. Like William Merritt Chase, Robert Henri, and John Singer Singer Sargent, I use black in flesh tones. (See the discussion of my premixed neutrals that follows.)

Permalba White. The white I use is Permalba white, manufactured by the F. Weber Company. It has a wonderful, soft, flowing texture and is very opaque. Permalba is also the basic element in my premixed flesh colors. As a result, they also have the smooth, easy, flowing quality that is such a pleasure in oil painting.

CHOOSING A PERSONAL PALETTE
Before we leave the traditional colors, I would like to say a few words about your own choice of colors. I realize that the colors on an artist's palette are as personal as his choice of clothing. There are more than 300 dif-

15. PALETTE CHART
This chart gives you a closer look at the arrangement of oil colors on my palette. Later in this chapter you will find a description of the standard colors on my palette and an explanation of the composition of my premixed colors, sold in tubes under the label John Howard Sanden Pro Mix Oil Colors.

ferent manufactured colors from which to choose, but most artists narrow them down to about a dozen. The choice of colors comes from experience of working with different colors and from close study of other artists' palettes. My teacher, Samuel Oppenheim, made a great study of the paintings of Velasquez and Sargent and could say with great authority, after putting his nose against a canvas hanging in the Metropolitan Museum, "He mixed that tone with yellow ochre, vermilion (vermilion has been widely replaced in contemporary use by cadmium red light), and a touch of white," and so on. With a few minor variations, my palette is very close to the one he suggested to his students at the Art Students League.

HISTORY OF MY PREMIXED PORTRAIT COLORS

Since I always like to be completely ready when my sitters come to the studio, for years I would spend an hour or so before the arrival of a sitter mixing combinations of flesh tones that I was reasonably certain I would need during the sitting. Once the basic flesh colors had been mixed, I could quickly and efficently alter these colors to meet my needs without losing valuable painting time. (Having key tones on hand prepared in quantity is basic to the premier coup technique and is described at great length in Chapter 6.)

It occurred to me that it would be wonderful to have the basic flesh tones ready in tubes, and so I soon began mixing quantities of flesh tones and tubing them myself. After many a Saturday afternoon spent mixing colors in the studio, I finally decided to find a manufacturer to help. The Martin/F. Weber Company in Philadelphia agreed to take the job and to manufacture and distribute the mixtures under the label "John Howard Sanden's Pro Mix Color System" (Figure 16).

16. THE "PRO MIX" PORTRAIT OIL COLORS
These premixed portrait colors, sold in a ten-tube set, are manufactured by the Martin/F. Weber Company in Philadelphia. They may be purchased by direct mail from National Art Seminars Corporation, Washington, Connecticut 06794.

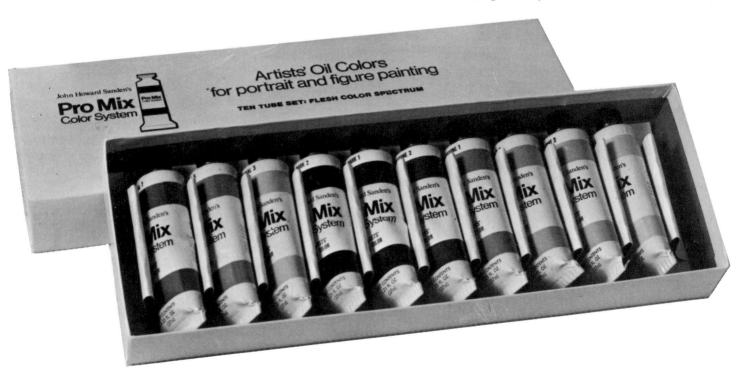

MIXING THE "PRO MIX" COLORS

I have always regretted the promotional trade name "Pro Mix" because it makes the colors sound like a gimmick. But these paints are merely basic mixtures that anyone can arrive at by combining the standard colors on the palette. Although they are time-savers and may help your color mixtures from becoming too cool or too warm, they are *not* magic potions. For the most part, each mixture consists largely of Permalba white. The following is a brief description of the standard colors you can mix to arrive at the Pro Mix colors.

Light 1. This is a clear, clean mixture that may be used for the lightest highlights on Caucasian skin. It can be mixed from the standard colors of white, yellow ochre, and cadmium red light.

Light 2. This mixture may be considered a basic flesh tone for Caucasian skin, although of course it has to be altered to meet each particular situation. It is darker, warmer, and grayer than Light 1. The mixture is made from white, yellow ochre, and cadmium red light, with cerulean blue added.

Light 3. A warm, pink color that may be used for ruddy flesh areas, this mixture is also made of white, yellow ochre, cadmium red light, and cerulean blue.

Halftone 1. Originally called "cool halftone," this mixture is basically used to indicate receding planes in the head. It is a mixture of white, yellow ochre, viridian, and cadmium red light.

Halftone 2. This warm, dark halftone is often used in those areas of the head where the light and shadow areas meet. It is a mixture of white, yellow ochre, cadmium red light, chromium oxide green, and cadmium orange.

Dark 1. A basic shadow tone for Caucasian skin and a good basic flesh color for dark-skinned subjects, this is a mixture of burnt sienna, white, viridian, and cadmium orange.

Dark 2. A darker tint than Dark 1, this is used for darkest accents in shadow areas. The mixture consists of burnt sienna, viridian, and cadmium orange.

Along with these basic flesh tones, I have found that the addition of three neutral colors helps me to quickly reduce the intensity of and neutralize both the standard palette colors and the premixed ones. Since few colors in real life match the intensity of the pigments as they come directly from the paint tube, these gray colors help me to adjust the palette colors to more natural, realistic tones.

Neutral 3. This mixture is a rather light, warm gray made of white, yellow ochre, and ivory black. It would fall on a value scale from 1 (white) to 9 (black) at position 3.

Neutral 5. A value in the middle between black and white, this mixture is also made from white, yellow ochre, and ivory black.

Neutral 7. A warm, dark gray at value 7 on the value scale, this mixture consists of white, ivory black, and raw sienna—the only color not on my standard palette.

There are three ways to prepare these colors. One way is to mix them in small quantities prior to each day's painting. Another method is to prepare a sufficient quantity to fill a set of "pound" tubes, and the third is to purchase the John Howard Sanden Pro Mix colors already made.

If you prefer to mix and tube your own colors, you will find the procedure described in detail in my first book, *Painting the Head in Oil.* This description includes precise formulas (page 57) and a pictorial demonstration of the method of preparation (pages 58–59).

My Pro Mix colors may be purchased either in convenient ten-tube boxed sets or, by the tube, from National Art Seminars Corporation, Washington, Connecticut 06794. Current price information may be obtained by writing to this company.

USING THE PREMIXED PORTRAIT COLORS

Remember that the premixed colors should be used like all the other colors on your palette. They are squeezed out of the tube and are ready to be mixed and adjusted to match the color and value you see before you. They are rarely used directly from the tube, but often they may be made suitable with the addition of one color, thus saving you the time of mixing three or four different colors together first. And, as I have already stated, having large quantities of each mixture allows you to paint in a thick, flowing, premier coup technique.

To gain familiarity with the range of variations possible with the premixed colors, I suggest that you practice the mixing exercises shown in *Painting the Head in Oil* (pages 64–66). The object of the exercises is to take each of the seven premixed colors and include just enough of the suggested additive to create a subtle variation. Remember that the color changes in the painting of flesh are extremely subtle and delicate.

Creating and Using Reference Material

2

Ever since artists have been challenged by the desire to produce realistic drawings, they have attempted to master the problem of accuracy in drawing by a wide variety of means. Lords and ladies would sit for endless hours while their images were sketched. Sometimes they were seated behind large squared off grids of fine cord that would enable the artist to properly proportion the drawing. Such "drawing machines," and the camera obscura, an astronomer's tool later used by artists, came into use as early as the sixteenth century as a means of increasing the accuracy and thoroughness of drawing.

When photography was discovered in 1839, it was immediately recognized that this discovery would have far-reaching implications for artists. Most painters saw the new picture-making process as a dangerous enemy. Others saw it at once as a wonderful convenience and assistance to their work. Those who predicted that photography would kill traditional portrait painting have been shown to be wrong, for portraiture has survived and is flourishing in the late twentieth century. Many portraitists have incorporated the most useful features of photography into their difficult art as helpful tools. The Impressionist painters immediately saw the advantage of the camera's ability to instantly record transitory effects of nature and to store vast amounts of visual information in a single instantaneous image. Edouard Manet, Edgar Degas, James Tissot, Henri de Toulouse-Lautrec, Paul Cézanne, among the French, and Americans Theodore Robinson and Thomas Eakins, for example, all painted with the aid of photographs. And I suspect that far more of the Impressionists used photographic reference material than we have been led to believe. Two books on the subject, *The Painter and the Photograph* by Van Deren Coke and *Art and Photography* by Aaron Scharf (see Suggested Reading) present an extremely interesting history of the use of photography in art.

A painter who uses photography as an aid must be sensitive to its advantages and disadvantages, be trained in its proper use, and also be aware of how to interpret photographic material from a painter's viewpoint. Photography must not be used in place of the intense observation that is the basis of painting from life but as a means to more creative and interesting work.

ADVANTAGES OF PHOTOGRAPHY IN PORTRAITURE
It seems to me that the camera offers five principal benefits to the painter.

1. *Recording Information.* The camera "freezes" a vast amount of visual detail instantly and accurately, and this can become a tremendous re-

source for the painter, if he is willing to learn how to edit and interpret the information.

2. *Allowing Experimentation with the Pose.* The time-consuming work of endless pose sketches can be reduced to a brief photographic sitting in which many angles and positions are explored without major commitments by the artist or the sitter. The artist is free to study a wide variety of possibilities and come to the next sitting with sound ideas for the most attractive pose.

3. *Permitting a Natural, Informal Expression and Manner.* This is perhaps the greatest advantage of photography for the portrait artist. The wooden expressions in so many old portraits are the result of long, tedious sittings. The painter who knows how to use a camera can record attractive, natural attitudes and expressions, freezing them instantaneously on film.

4. *Allowing Work Without the Sitter's Presence.* With the aid of good photographs to assist recall, a painter can continue to work after a sitter has left the studio.

5. *Reinforcing Visual Impressions.* Not only can the camera assist the artist in retaining the image of the sitter once the sitter is gone, but it can also help the artist see elusive characteristics—such as a hard-to-hold expression—when the sitter is present.

I feel that the modern technology of photography is invaluable to the conscientious painter and that a painter who does not make good use of it is like a surgeon who refuses to use X rays because it would be "cheating" to know what he was looking for before cutting! However, a painter cannot merely copy a photograph any more than a surgeon can consider his work done once he has seen the problem on the X-ray film.

A painter must make careful, sensitive, interpretive use of his reference material. The qualities that make or break a painting are timeless and independent of the methods involved in the actual painting process. The painting must stand as a work of art, a tangible by-product of the artist's life and spirit, long after the practical work itself is accomplished.

PHOTOGRAPHIC EQUIPMENT

I will now discuss the photographic equipment and procedures I employ and my reasons for these choices. This brings us to the first rule: if you intend to use photographic reference material in your portrait work, *you must take the photographs yourself.* You cannot work meaningfully from someone else's snapshots! Your photography must be a part of your creative process. And here is the second rule: you must standardize your technical procedure so that the complexities won't overwhelm you. Once you have mastered a standard photographic procedure, you are free to concentrate on the creative aspects of pose, lighting, and arrangement. So the camera becomes an extension of yourself. The camera, lights, and film are merely tools in the hands of a creative artist. The final painting is what matters. The camera merely increases the creative possibilities.

My photographic equipment is shown in Figure 17 and will be described below.

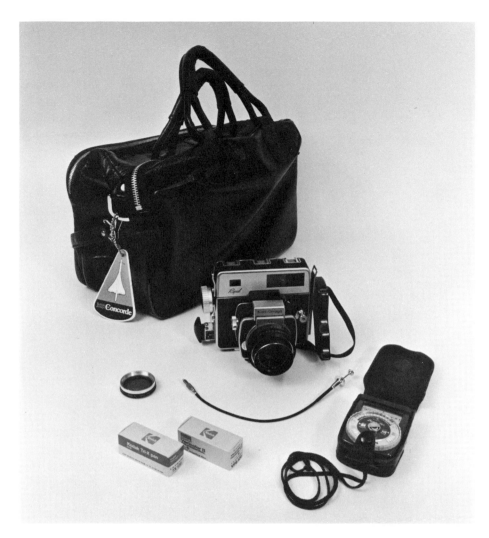

17. CAMERA AND SUPPLIES
Pictured here are: (A) An all-purpose carry bag. (B) Koni-Omega Rapid Camera (now called the Rapid Omega) with a 90 mm Super Omega lens. It has a 2¼ x 2¾" (5.7 x 7 cm) professional format and yields ten exposures on standard 120-roll film. (C) 80A blue filter, which must be used with Vericolor film. (D) Films: Kodak Tri-X (black-and-white film, ASA 400) and Kodak Vericolor II, Type S (color negative film, ASA 100). (E) Cable release. (F) Gossen Luna-Pro Exposure Meter.

The Camera. The selection of a camera is a very personal matter. There are so many to choose from, and they are all remarkable devices. I prefer a 120mm format, although I am aware that the 35mm camera is very popular and convenient. The main reason I prefer the larger format is that the negative size (2¼ x 2¾") gives me contact proofs that are large enough to edit without magnification. I often find that the best pose or attitude of my subject will literally "jump out" at me from a page of these contact proofs. I have also found that if I study the proofs too long and too closely, my first spontaneous reaction is lost. Figure 18 shows a sheet of contact proofs that demonstrates the camera's ability to record a variety of poses effortlessly, in a brief time. The camera I use is called the Rapid Omega and is made by Konica. There are numerous lenses available to use interchangeably with this excellent camera, but for years I have used the camera's original, standard 90mm lens.

Exposure Meter. After the camera, the exposure meter is perhaps the most valuable item in your equipment bag. It pays to invest in a good one! There are several outstanding models. I use the Gossen Luna-Pro.

Films. I use two films: Tri-X for black-and-white prints and Vericolor S for color prints. I concentrate on the black-and-white film because I find this to be by far the most valuable reference source. The color prints are so

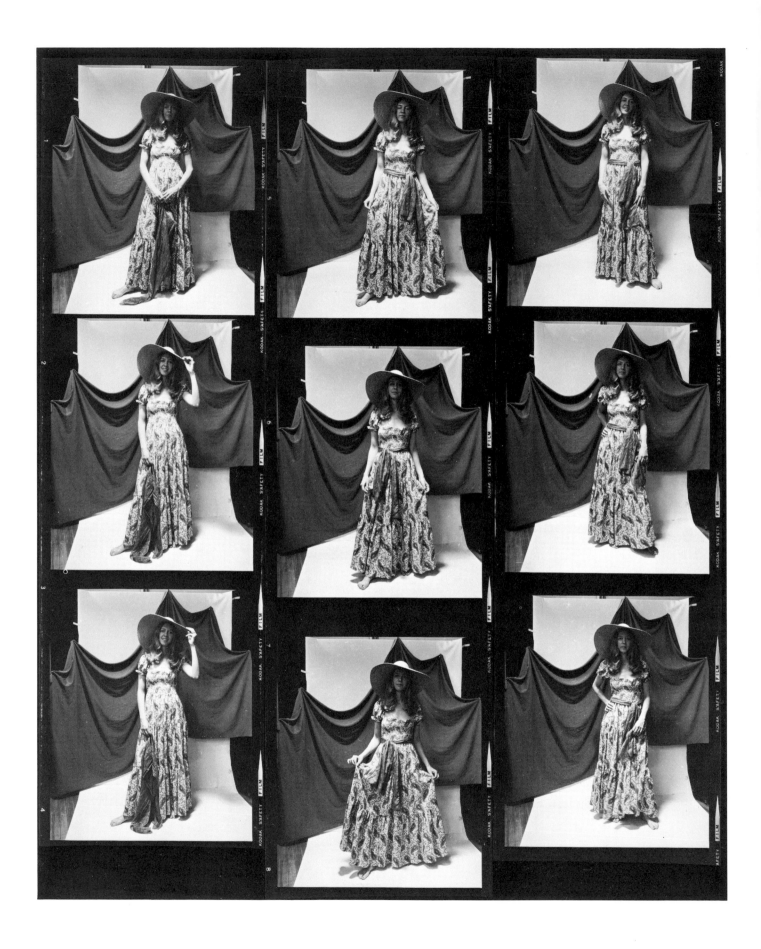

prone to subjective variation on the part of the lab technicians that they are almost worthless for my purposes. Instead, I rely on my own observation of the sitter for color.

Miscellaneous. When you want to isolate your subject from a specific setting, you will probably want to have some kind of easily portable background screen. In my trunk of equipment, I have a homemade unit consisting of two lightweight folding light stands for the verticals and a sectional curtain rod for the crossbar. You also should have a cable release for your camera to avoid camera movement and perhaps two "gobos"—devices to block out the light from specific areas. Gobos can be as simple as squares of cardboard clipped to a light stand. Be sure to carry three 25-foot (7.6m) extension cords and some conversion adapters so that your three-prong equipment will plug into old-fashioned two-prong outlets, if necessary. To carry all of this, I have a trunk mounted on sturdy wheels. A word of caution: the entire apparatus, including the trunk, must weigh less than 70 pounds or the airlines may not accept it as luggage.

LIGHTING

I take the task of lighting *very* seriously and consider it one of the most important aspects of my work. Figure 19 illustrates the simple, convenient set of portable lighting equipment I employ. There are three lights: a main light, a fill-in light, and an accent light.

Main Light. My main light is a Reflectasol Soff-Box with a 25" (64 cm) outside measurement. The light fixture is a Smith-Victor model 770 Quartz Broad with a DYH tungsten-halogen lamp.

Fill-in Light. For a fill-in light I use a 36" (91 cm) umbrella on a Reflectasol clamp and bracket. The light is a Colortran Quartz-King 650, which uses an FAD tungsten halogen lamp.

Accent Light. My accent light is a Smith-Victor model 760 with a DYH lamp. Surrounding the lamp are folding shades—called "barndoors"—that allow me to concentrate the light.

ARRANGING THE LIGHTING

There are two ways to light the subject. One is to use the existing light in your studio or the existing light found on location in your subject's home or office. The other way is by utilizing portable electronic lighting that can be directed and controlled by the artist. To say that one is natural and the other artificial is nonsense. One comes from the sun, the other comes from electrical energy, and they are both very real. But while I can't control the sun, I have complete control over the electric light I use.

Placing the Main Light. To determine how close to the subject the main light should be, you must study the effect of its brightness on the subject's face. If the light is too far away, the effect will be too dull. If it's too close, the "specular highlights"—bright highlight spots—will be too intense and the shadows will be too harsh. You will eventually determine the best po-

18. CONTACT PROOFS (opposite page) This sheet of contact proofs shows how a variety of poses can be explored in a short period of time. The 120mm camera produces proofs that are 2¼ x 2¾" (5.7 x 7 cm), large enough to be easily studied without the aid of a magnifying glass.

19. STUDIO LIGHTS

The three lights pictured here are: (A) Fill-in Light. The stand consists of a PIC castor-base tripod, model HD-1; a Reflectasol clamp and bracket; and a 36" umbrella. The light is a Colortran Quartz-King 650 with a FAD tungsten-halogen (3200K) lamp. (B) Accent Light. The stand is the same as (A). The light is Smith-Victor model 760 and the lamp is a DYH tungsten-halogen (3200K) bulb with barndoors. (C) Two scrims—for use with B to reduce the intensity of my accent light (B). (D) Main Light. I use a 25" (63.5 cm) Reflectasol Soff-Box. The light is a Smith-Victor model 770, and the lamp, a DYH tungsten-halogen (3200K) bulb.

sition for your purpose through experience as you note the effects of the lighting on your film. As a general rule, however, the main light is placed about 5 feet (1.5 m) from the subject.

Apart from the distance between the light and the subject, you must determine its angle in relation to the face, since this will affect the location of the shadows. The shadow treatment that best suits a particular model and pose is both complicated and subjective. You'll have to experiment with a variety of shadow patterns and with lighting of various types and intensities to find the one that will enhance your subject's best qualities.

For a start, keep in mind that a strong, simple, soft-edged light from a three-quarter position, with good, firm shadows, is usually best. The lighting need not—indeed, should not—be complicated.

Placing the Fill-in Light. The fill-in light is used to raise the value of (lighten) the shadows. Without this light, the shadows on your photographic prints would be dense and black and completely without detail. The position of the fill-in light depends on the intensity of the lamps—a photographer will speak at this point of light-to-shadow ratios. For example, a 3:1 ratio is considered optimum, with the main light being three times as intense as the fill-in light.

Of course, you will not be thinking in these analytical, mathematical terms. It is *how it looks* that matters. And only experience will tell you how your equipment should be used to achieve the desired effect. I usually position my umbrella fill-in light quite a long way from the subject, sometimes as far as 20 feet (6.1 m).

Placing the Accent Light. The accent light is used to direct the eye to specific areas on the model. I have always admired the rather unconventional effects Sir William Orpen, the great English portraitist, achieved in many of his portraits—for example, light coming from mysterious off-stage sources and sparkling along the contour of a face or a sleeve. I don't know how Orpen achieved these effects (perhaps by artful use of the windows and screens in his studio), but I have always enjoyed experimenting with similar effects, using my small quartz lamp as an accent light. Sometimes a crisp illumination of the side of a face will bring the subject out from the background. Sometimes just a touch of light on the back of the hair will add interest and animation. If you use this third light, the accent light, use it with discretion and use it conservatively.

STANDARDIZE YOUR PROCEDURE
Once again, if you are going to use photography, I urge you to standardize your equipment and procedure. Find a good simple system that works for you and master its use until it is second nature. Remember that you are a painter and that you're merely using photography as a tool. Standardization does not make you an automaton. Just the opposite! It frees you to concentrate on your creativity, with poses and ideas. You want to concentrate on the sitter, not on the mechanics of what you are doing.

I am always impressed by stories of the great Canadian photographer Yousef Karsh, who strives to make his camera and lights as unobtrusive as possible. He and the subject sit facing each other engaged in personal conversation. When the right moment—the magic moment—comes, the photographer squeezes the cable release, which snaps the shutter unnoticed in the shadows behind him. As an artist, you must always strive to snap the hidden shutter and then go on to record your most intimate reactions to the subject through your paintbrush.

PROBLEMS IN INTERPRETING PHOTOGRAPHIC MATERIAL
When you begin to think of your photographs as creative resource material and not just as something to copy, you will be a long way toward the successful incorporation of photography into the creative rhythm of your artistic life. There are, however, specific problems as well as advantages that you must be aware of when using photographic reference material.

1. *Distortion of Shapes.* Unless you are careful, the camera can give you real problems here. In portraiture, the most obvious one is that objects nearer to the picture plane are often exaggerated in size. For example, a hand extended toward the camera can appear positively huge in the photographic print.

The two technical steps to avoid this type of size distortion are: first, keeping the camera far enough away from the subject (the greater the distance between the camera and the subject, the less the distortion), and second, using increased focal length lenses. The best safeguard against

A

B

20. THREE DENSITIES FROM ONE NEGATIVE

These three photographs show the remarkable range of densities that can be printed from a single negative. It is often valuable to make all three. (A) A normal density print (above) will give information on the middle values. (B) A light print (above right) will reveal detail in the darks. (For example, here we can now see clearly into the eyes and into the shadows of the beard and collar.) (C) A dark print (right) will increase the visibility of the highlights. Printing all three densities will compensate somewhat for the camera's insensitivity to values. Of course, the human eye is sensitive to all these details simultaneously.

C

photographic distortion, of course, is simply a well-trained artist's eye. The camera cannot trick the artist trained through years of traditional academic drawing and observation of proportions.

2. *Flattening of Forms.* This is one of the most distressing shortcomings of the photographic image. Forms that appear richly dimensional to the eye appear strangely flat and dull in a photograph. Once again, the cure is personal observation and sensitivity to the subject when he or she is present.

3. *Distortion of Values.* The lens is not nearly as sensitive as your eyes. The evidence for this is the simple fact that you need far more light to expose your films properly than you do for normal vision. The range of value perception is not nearly as large or as subtle as that of which your eyes are capable. Tonal relationships are often harsh and contrasty in photographs, and the lower values—the dark tones—are usually much darker in the photographic print than they appear to the eye. In fact, to produce a full range of tonal values, I have my darkroom technician make several prints from each negative: a "normal" print for the middle values, a light print to show detail in the dark tones, and a dark print to show detail in the lightest values. In other words, it is often necessary to make three prints from the same negative to reveal all the information that your eyes see so effortlessly. A set of these three different prints is shown in Figure 20.

NOW FOR THE PLUSES
In spite of the shortcomings, there are many advantages.

1. *Selecting the Best Elements.* When I use photography in portraiture, I take a really generous supply of pictures—maybe 80 to 100 exposures of one subject. Later, as I am developing the painting, if I decide to change the position of a hand, I may find just the pose I want in one of my proofs. Or I may have a photograph of a superb head with just the expression I want, but I need to go back and rephotograph the pose of the hands in order to combine the two in my final composition. So, in exploring the possibilities my reference material offers, I keep in mind the options of selecting and combining several photographs.

2. *Redesigning the Elements.* As I build the picture, I feel free to move the various elements anywhere I wish. A vase of flowers can be shifted from side to side, raised, or lowered. The patterns of a background can be eliminated entirely. Details can be edited out as I see fit. In short, I have the same freedoms when working from photographs that I do when working from life.

3. *Adjusting Color.* When I work from life, I feel duty-bound to paint the colors exactly as I see them before me. So if the model is wearing a red dress, I feel that I can only paint it red—I couldn't possibly paint it green. But when I have a black-and-white photograph before me, I can paint the dress any color I wish to suit the requirements of my composition.

In Figures 21 and 22, I will show you some photographic examples and how they were translated into paint.

21. THE PAINTING AND THE PHOTOGRAPH

The essence of a subject may be captured with far less detail than a photograph reveals. This is the wonderful advantage of a painting. The artist may reveal in a painting all that is necessary to tell the story without having to record every minute detail. A painter who uses photographic reference material must be able to "read" the photograph sensitively and accurately. Here, my impression of this gracious and beautiful lady is told by the painting, not by the photograph.

22. THE PAINTING AND THE PHOTOGRAPH

The photograph of this distinguished scientist-editor had the effect of widening and flattening the face. In the painting, you can see that the face is slimmed down. The sittings from life showed the eyes to be much more intense than the photograph portrays, and the crispness of the mouth was also accentuated. The overly busy detail of the tie in the photograph has been subdued, and the hair, which of course changes with each sitting, is "fluffed-up" a bit in the painting. The painting is my impression of the sitter. The photograph is merely a record of a moment in time.

Part II
Creating the Portrait

An artist's work "should proceed in accordance with a well thought-out plan. A haphazard approach is practically certain to result in failure, just as it would in any other line. Yet some young [artists] foolishly start work at once upon the canvas, blindly trusting to some kind of providence to guide the arm. The canvas shouldn't be touched until one knows exactly what he wants to put on it. . . ." (From *Norman Rockwell, Illustrator*, by Arthur Guptill. New York: Watson-Guptill, 1946, p. 54.)

Having spent many years as an illustrator, I have always had great admiration for Norman Rockwell and feel that the preceding advice he gives to young illustrators applies just as well to portrait painting. *The path to a successful portrait is thorough preplanning.* If the elements of a portrait have been carefully planned in advance of execution, the portrait has a much greater chance of success.

The procedure I normally use in carrying out a portrait assignment is a practical approach that, if carefully followed, will go a long way toward ensuring the success of the finished portrait. Once again, the basis of the approach described here is thorough preliminary planning. All details of the painting are established before the final canvas is begun.

I don't expect every artist who reads this book to adopt my procedure without question. Far from it! But I have followed this procedure in the creation of hundreds of portraits and can testify that it works. Let me describe my portrait procedure in detail. Then you can select the features that appeal to you and perhaps adapt or discard the others. By studying the work and methods of various artists, you'll eventually develop your own style and procedure.

3

The Planning Meeting

Before the sittings actually begin, it is advisable to meet with your sitter and client for about an hour to work out preliminary decisions. My first meeting with the subject—and client, if possible—is informal and is held in the subject's home or office. Meeting the subject gives me a chance to get a few ideas or reinforce those I may already have about the portrait.

Topics discussed at the planning meeting include the function or purpose of the portrait, the spirit or mood of the work, and its size. These decisions will determine the costume to be worn to the first sitting and will influence the background or setting of the portrait as well. A schedule of sittings is also established at this time, if possible.

Figure 23 contains a list of the preliminary decisions made during the planning meeting. I suggest that you review it before you go to the meeting—but don't bring it with you. You can fill it out later, when you return to the studio. Do take a tape measure with you to the meeting, however, to measure the dimensions of the area where the portrait will hang. Bring your portfolio (see Chapter 8) along with you too. The portfolio may spark some good ideas for you and the client and may help you gain his confidence.

As you and the subject discuss these basic matters, you will have the opportunity to study your subject's natural gestures, poses, and expressions. Be alert and sensitive to your subject's personality and make mental notes that will help you cue your sitter when he comes to the model stand. Posing for an artist is a unique and sometimes slightly unnerving experience, and even prominent people who are used to being in control of most situations may stiffen at the first sitting. But the more you get to know your sitter, the easier will be the rapport between you. Here are some of the items you'll be resolving during the planning meeting.

FUNCTION OF THE PORTRAIT

The main purpose of a portrait is to bring pleasure to those who commissioned it. And what prompted the portrait to be painted in the first place is its function. It may be a gift of affection, a private family portrait, a business or official portrait, a memorial or posthumous portrait, or a combination of these items. Whatever the reason, you should know the function of the portrait in advance, since it will most certainly influence the spirit of the work. For instance, if the portrait of a man is commissioned as a private family gift, you may want to portray the subject in casual clothes, or outdoors, or with a suggestion of how he spends time with his family. On the other hand, if the same man's company commissioned his portrait, he would no doubt be portrayed in a more formal setting, probably in business attire.

MR. EDWARD S. PINNEY (overleaf)
Oil on canvas, 30 x 25" (76 x 64 cm), collection Mrs. Pinney. Mr. Pinney had an outstanding career as an attorney with one of the great New York law firms, in addition to wide activities in civic and philanthropic affairs. He loved his books and had a great library in his country home. The astrolabe that occupies the table beside him was a fascinating detail to paint. It was the visit to the beautiful Pinney country estate in Connecticut that prompted my wife and me to buy a home in the same community, one of Connecticut's most picturesque areas.

23. THE PLANNING CHECKLIST: PRELIMINARY DECISIONS (opposite page) This form will help you make important decisions during the planning meeting.

THE PRELIMINARY DECISIONS

The artist settles these matters
in consultation with his client.

THE PLANNING
CHECKLIST

The Function of the Portrait

The purpose of the portrait is
- ☐ A gift of affection
- ☐ A private, family portrait
- ☐ A business portrait
- ☐ An official portrait
- ☐ A memorial portrait

The Spirit of the Portrait

1. What is to be the clothing worn by the subject? _____

_____

2. Is the mood to be formal or informal? _____

_____

The Size of the Portrait

1. How much of the subject is to be included?
   - ☐ Head and shoulders
     (Possibly 20"x16")
   - ☐ Head, shoulders, upper torso
     (Possibly 24"x20")
   - ☐ Head, shoulders, down to the waist
     (Possibly 30"x25")
   - ☐ Including hands (three-quarter length)
     (Possibly 36"x30")
   - ☐ Larger three-quarter
     (Possibly 42"x35")
   - ☐ Full length
     (Possibly 90"x46")

2. What will the background be? _____

_____

3. Where will the painting hang? _____

_____

4. The price of the painting is $_____

In the memorial or posthumous portrait, the artist must decide whether to accept the job after viewing the collection of photographs that are available. I am willing to do posthumous portraits if there is a good studio portrait photograph of the subject available. I am not a magician, however, and will usually refuse a job when the client has *only* a collection of candid snapshots. My conception of the person will probably not coincide with his loved ones' version, and I just don't like to try it.

I recently had a job that began as a gift family portrait, but my subject, a distinguished elderly man, became ill and died before the first sitting. Fortunately, his wife had a fine studio portrait photograph of him and his son together, and I was able to paint the man's portrait using this photograph as my main reference. Her collection of snapshots was a wonderful reinforcement for the work—the man was extremely active and many of the snapshots portrayed him outdoors on his ranch—but the key to my portrait was this one photograph. On the other hand, had he lived long enough to sit for the work, I might have chosen a completely different pose and setting. (The final painting is reproduced on page 110, in the color section on painting technique.)

SPIRIT OF THE PORTRAIT

The spirit of the portrait is determined partly by the function of the portrait and partly through conversation with the sitter and client. A personal chat will often reveal much about the sitter that will help the artist decide if the mood of the painting is to be formal or informal and will alert him to what the subject intends to wear for the sittings. Clothing and setting will have an effect on the overall spirit of the portrait, as will the attitude of the pose. For instance, a portrait commissioned as a business portrait may have as its subject a man who is relaxed and at ease in a casual pose. If the setting is to be a business office, you might alter a formal mood by having the subject perched on the side of his desk in a casual pose. Or if you have a commission for a private family portrait of a woman from a family that has a traditionally formal lifestyle, you would want the spirit of the portrait to be formal and would probably portray the subject in a formal gown.

The spirit of the portrait will also be influenced by the value and color plan that you work out for the portrait. These aspects will be discussed later, but the meetings with the client and subject will most likely influence the mood that you, the artist, will convey in these aspects of the painting. For example, a subject wearing a dark outfit and painted in a dark background will probably suggest a formal mood or spirit. The portraits on pages 46–47 illustrate a wide variety of functions and moods.

SIZE OF THE PORTRAIT

Several factors may influence the size of a portrait. The most important one is the size of the image. The traditional image size in portraiture is lifesize or near lifesize. This permits the most effective recreation of the subject. For a standing portrait, where the subject is right up to the picture plane (that is, in the foreground), a full lifesize image can and should be used. If the subject is seated with knees facing the viewer, allowance must be made for the fact that the head is now recessed into the background to some extent. In this case, the effect of perspective dictates that the head—which is now somewhat farther from the viewer—should be slightly

MR. HARRY A. JACOBS, JR.
Oil on canvas, 30 x 25" (76 x 64 cm), collection The Bache Group, New York. Mr. Jacobs is chairman of a Wall Street brokerage house. Since I was working on a rather small canvas, I chose this seated pose to bring the hands into the composition.

THE FUNCTION AND
SPIRIT OF THE PORTRAIT

MR. GEORGE LAMADE
Oil on canvas, 30 x 25" (76 x 64 cm), collection Grit Publishing Company. This posthumous portrait of the well-known publisher was based on a handsome tintype, which was crisp in detail and striking in lighting. I was inspired by the photograph, and painted with a directness and boldness that matches some of my best work from life.

MR. ROBERT SCHEU
Oil on canvas, 38 x 32" (96 x 81 cm), collection Marine Midland Bank, Buffalo. This was an official bank portrait, but since Mr. Scheu had already retired and was enjoying life on his sailboat, we decided to depart from a formal office setting and show him outdoors.

DR. WILLIAM S. PETTIT
Oil on canvas, 44½ x 42" (113 x 107 cm), collection Ursinus College. This is an official university portrait designed to hang in a prominent spot in the library. Dr. Pettit was as energetic and enthusiastic a subject as he was an educator, and I wanted to show that he was always "on the go," hence this rather informal pose.

MR. EARL T. BARNES
Oil on canvas, 48 x 40" (122 x 102 cm), collection Mr. and Mrs. Barnes. This portrait was a family gift that everyone wanted to be informal. Here is a case where the size of the portrait was increased by the addition of the well-loved family pet.

STANDARD SIZES

24 x 20″ (61 x 51 cm). BILL
Oil on canvas. This size is considered a standard size for a head and shoulders and may include some of the upper torso. I use this size primarily for sketches done in preparation for the final canvas, or for demonstration sketches for my students as is this one of Bill Pease, one of my monitors at The Art Students League. A head and shoulders can also be 20 x 16″ (51 x 41 cm).

30 x 25″ (76 x 64 cm). MR. JAMES HALL BROOKS
Oil on canvas. This standard size should include hands, however you usually have to think of a way of getting the hands above waist level. By having Mr. Brooks hold his hat, I was able to include one hand and balance the composition. It is often difficult to make an interesting composition in this small size, but try to avoid what I call the "pop-up," when the subject's hands are at his side and only head, shoulders, and upper torso show.

36 x 30" (91 x 76 cm). DR. RUDOLPH BAER
Oil on canvas. Collection N.Y.U. Medical School. This stand-
ard size portrait gives you enough room to allow space around
your sitter and an interesting pose of the hands. You'll probably
be able to find stock frames in this size although I always have my
frames custom made for each portrait.

42 x 34" (107 x 86 cm). MR. JACK ARON
Oil on canvas, collection Tulane University. Once you get larger
than 36 x 30" (91 x 76 cm), there are really no specific standard
sizes. All frames have to be custom made. The size shown here is a
good one for allowing plenty of space around the subject.

MR. DAVID LAUB
*Oil on canvas, 36 x 30" (91 x 76 cm), collection Marine Midland Bank, Buffalo. Since Mr. Laub
was instrumental in acquiring a distinguished collection of contemporary art for the banking
firm he headed, it seemed only natural to use this striking ceramic mural as a background for his
portrait. To create a proper tonal foil for the head, I subdued the bold primary colors of the mural
and reduced the contrasts there.*

smaller than it would be if the subject were standing and thus closer to the viewer.

Almost all adult human head sizes fall somewhere between 8 and 10" (20 to 25 cm), and Sargent had a rather general rule that head size should be "the size shown by the calipers, minus half an inch." In an official portrait, however, the head size may be as large as 10" (25 cm), to suggest heroic qualities. Whenever possible, I like to have the freedom to determine the exact dimensions myself so I have complete control over this aspect of the composition.

The size of the painting may also be influenced by props or animals the subject may wish to include in the background. Since I base my prices only on the number of *human* subjects included in the painting, there is no additional charge for this. And I am always glad to include a family pet or special prop because it makes my job more interesting and often presents a new challenge.

Here is a typical example of how props can add interest to a painting. One of my subjects, Mr. David Laub (opposite), was enthusiastically involved with the modern art collection purchased by his bank, and so we decided to include a striking ceramic mural as a background for the painting. In this case, the design did not alter the size but was worked into the predetermined 36 x 30" (91 x 76 cm) size.

The space in which a painting will hang—such as over a fireplace or in a boardroom—is often determined in advance by the client and will affect the size of the painting. In the case of a boardroom portrait, you'll need to know the sizes of existing portraits and whether they are all uniform or varying in size. In a situation like this, it is a good idea to visit the room and take measurements before beginning the painting so you'll know the outer limits of the size. But I'm not normally too influenced by the decor of a room, because a portrait must stand alone as a piece of artwork, regardless of where it is hung.

The size of a painting also usually affects its price. A chart of typical sizes and prices will be shown later in the book, when I discuss the business side of portraiture. But meanwhile, in Figure 23, you will find a list of standard sizes and the extent of the subject's body generally included in each. Examples of typical-size paintings are also shown on pages 48–49. Although the size of the portrait is often based on price, I don't believe that price should be the main deciding factor. Instead, I feel that an artist must do the best job possible and so, even after the price is set, if you discover a larger canvas is called for, I think you should paint it without hesitation for the agreed-on price. I even allow for this change in size on the "Commission Details" form (see Chapter 9), where I list both a tentative size and the final one.

SCHEDULING FUTURE SITTINGS

A schedule for the rest of the sittings—at least a tentative one—is also established during the planning meeting, and the sitter is provided with a copy of the dates and times. When scheduling the sittings, remember: it's better to plan a number of short sittings than to have your sitter at the studio for long periods of time, since this is physically draining on the artist as well as the sitter. Unless there's a specific date on which the painting is due, based on an unveiling ceremony, a retirement, or other reason, it's almost impossible to set the date of the final sitting in advance.

MR. HUGH O. MACLELLAN
Oil on canvas, 40 x 30" (102 x 76 cm), collection Provident Life and Accident Insurance Company, Chattanooga. This portrait includes many of the features I like to include in a business portrait: informal pose, casual naturalness in expression, and simple background. This portrait is the same size as the companion portrait of Mr. Unruh (opposite), but the difference in pose permitted more "air" in this composition.

MR. HENRY C. UNRUH
Oil on canvas, 40 x 30" (102 x 76 cm), collection Provident Life and Accident Insurance Company, Chattanooga. Mr. Unruh is a tall and commanding figure, and the portrait would have been improved with a few inches more space around it, but the size was established by other portraits in the boardroom. A light-colored business suit is always pleasant to paint because the shapes and forms of the clothing are more visible there than on a dark suit.

24. FRAMING YOUR PORTRAITS

Here are four handsome styles, each ideal in its way for portraits:

(A) The "Gilbert Stuart," a traditional American pattern from Williamsburg, with crossed ribbons. Excellent for all portraits, ideal for a man's portrait. (Style DM 1183A.)

(B) A more contemporary style, designed by Elizabeth Sanden as a "reverse-cove" pattern, in which the thickest part of the frame is nearest the painting. (Style DM 2252.)

(C) The carved decoration at the corners makes this graceful pattern ideal for a woman's portrait. (Style DM 1218A.)

(D) The elegant curving design of this frame is French in origin. Shown here with a wide linen insert, this frame is also perfect for a woman's portrait. (Style 607.)

Styles A, B, and C are available from D. Matt, Inc., 223 East 80th Street, New York, N.Y. 10021. Style D is available from Melvin Picture Frame Company, Inc., 20 Marbledale Road, Tuckahoe, N.Y. 10707.

SELECTING A FRAME

You're probably wondering why this topic is appearing so early in the portrait painting procedure. The answer is simple: the frame is an integral part of the finished product, and I feel that it can make or break the final painting. I therefore discuss the frame with my client as early in the planning stages as possible and make a specific recommendation. This allows me to have the painting framed in time for the final sittings so that it seems complete when viewed by sitter or client. It also gives people a far better impression of the painting and allows me to make better painting judgments as the work nears completion. Therefore I advise you to select the frames for your portraits early and with care, and don't hesitate to recommend a certain style that you prefer to your client. Remember: the painting and frame are a unit and should always be considered together.

In selecting a frame, keep in mind the following: a traditional style of painting calls for a traditional frame, and a touch of carving always adds richness. A gilded finish, even gold leaf if the client will permit it, is usually best. If the finish is too strong for the effect you desire, ask your framer to apply a wash or toner to reduce its brightness. I prefer a finely hand-carved wooden frame and usually like to include a linen insert around the outside edge of the painting, just inside the frame (Figure 24). In fact, Elizabeth has designed a special pattern for our New York framer. If your price range doesn't allow for the finest quality frame, however, a good rule is to spend 10 to 15% of the cost of the painting on the frame. (The cost of framing is not included in the price of the portrait at the gallery through which I do most of my work.) In this case, it might be a good idea to raise your prices to cover the cost of a frame, so you never have to let a painting leave your studio unframed.

IN LIEU OF THE PLANNING MEETING

Sometimes, because of distance or lack of time, the planning meeting may take place only moments before the first sitting. When this occurs, Elizabeth has usually spoken with someone involved with the painting—a secretary or a spouse—and has made it clear that the sitter should be wearing the clothing in which he would like to be painted. But one of the reasons I prefer to have the planning meeting sometime before the first sitting is that it gives me a chance to have input on the costume chosen—the color and style of the dress—and it helps to conceptualize the portrait before the first sitting takes place.

4 Arranging the Composition

After the preliminary decisions have been made, the artist alone must determine a multitude of details (see Figure 25) that will influence the success of the portrait. Sometimes these decisions are not completely conscious ones, but all have an effect on the final results. Let's start with the obvious ones and then summarize the more complex aesthetic elements.

CHOOSING A POSE

The pose is the most obvious element of the composition and the first one I begin to arrange. Your earlier meeting with the subject should have served to give you some idea as to the pose you'll select. You must first decide if your subject will be seated or standing and then determine the angle of the head: full face, three-quarter from right or left, or profile.

Factors that may influence your choice of a seated or standing pose are (1) the stature of your subject and (2) canvas size limitations. For instance, a tall, regal subject might be shown to best advantage in a standing pose. Or, as I have already mentioned, a small canvas might force a seated pose in order to include the hands.

A seated pose will also require a proper chair. Although I have a collection of chairs in my studio, I invariably find that I never have the one that is *just right*. This is one reason why I like to work on location, where I can often use a handsome chair that the sitter finds both comfortable and of personal significance.

ANGLE OF THE HEAD

Selection of a pose also includes the choice of the angle of the sitter's face. I use photographs as one would use a sketchbook. My photography allows me to experiment rapidly with a number of different angles. If you have made a careful study of faces, you know that a person's face is often different when viewed from different sides and angles. For example, sometimes one eye or one corner of the mouth is noticeably lower than the other. A flattering angle can minimize unattractive differences or emphasize those that might make a particularly striking portrait. For example, you may want to picture someone with a prominent nose from a lower angle to minimize the length of the nose. The sitter may also prefer a particular viewpoint. So look carefully at your sitter, and—as Andrea Ericson, long-time director of Portraits Inc. so aptly quoted the song at our 1980 National Portrait Seminar, "Accentuate the positive, eliminate the negative, latch on to the affirmative, and don't mess with Mr. In-Between!"

25. THE PLANNING CHECKLIST: COMPOSITIONAL DECISIONS (opposite page)
This form will prepare you for the initial sittings and should help you to compose and plan your painting.

ARRANGING THE ELEMENTS

These are aesthetic decisions which are made by *the artist alone.*

The Pose

- ☐ Standing
- ☐ Seated
- ☐ Full face
- ☐ ¾ left
- ☐ ¾ right
- ☐ Profile

The Lighting

The painter's viewpoint is to be
- ☐ Shadow side
- ☐ Light side

The main light source will be
- ☐ Frontal
- ☐ From the left
- ☐ From the right
- ☐ High position
- ☐ Normal

The lighting will be
- ☐ Warm
- ☐ Cool
- ☐ Neutral
- ☐ Strong
- ☐ Subdued
- ☐ Broad
- ☐ Concentrated

The Tonal Plan

The general concept will be
- ☐ High key
- ☐ Low key
- ☐ Middle range

The background will be
- ☐ White
- ☐ Light halftone
- ☐ Middle tone
- ☐ Dark halftone
- ☐ Dark

Organizational Elements

The point of view
- ☐ Eye level
- ☐ Above eye level
- ☐ Below eye level

Distribution of shapes
- ☐ Size of the main subject relative to the space
- ☐ Placement of focal point
- ☐ Relative sizes of secondary subjects
- ☐ Overlapping
- ☐ Points of contact
- ☐ Providing an eye pathway

The Color Plan

- ☐ Dominant hue
- ☐ Analogous
- ☐ Complementary

POINT OF VIEW

The point of view is the perspective or eye level of the artist. I use an 18-inch (46 cm) model stand to bring a seated subject up to my eye level because this viewpoint seems to be ideal. It is also the most widely used point of view for achieving a realistic, natural-looking portrait.

Even though eye-level portraits are the most common, many excellent portraits have been painted from other vantage points. Examples in which the subject is below eye level—where the artist is looking down at the subject—are Sargent's portrait of Lady Meyer and her children and Boldini's portrait of Consuelo, Duchess of Marlborough, and her son. This point of view can allow the artist to achieve a novel intimacy of effect and an interesting flow of design.

You can also choose a low viewpoint, looking up at your subject, as Sargent did in his portrait of the Marlborough family. The low eye level gives an elevated, dignified, and rather auspicious aspect to the subjects.

At any rate, altering the eye level from the conventional eye-to-eye level may cause distortions in a portrait, so proceed with caution in choosing an unusual vantage point. But do be aware of the possibilities.

DISTRIBUTING THE SHAPES

In positioning your subject on the canvas, you must always be aware of the abstract pattern of the positive shapes (your subject and props) and the negative shapes of the surrounding canvas (Figure 26). If you make the subject lifesize, which is most advisable, then the size of the shapes around the subject will, of course, be determined by the size of the canvas itself. Whatever your decision, you must always be aware of the space in which your subject "moves."

Since the focal point in a portrait is always the head, its placement in relation to the entire canvas must also be carefully considered. It is better to place the head slightly off center than smack in the middle of your canvas. But how far to the right or left should be determined by the pose of the hands and body and the direction the head is facing. For example, if the subject's head is turned slightly to the right, you may want to place the head to the left of center on the canvas.

LIGHTING THE STUDIO

A number of important decisions must be made concerning the general lighting of the portrait studio. Before electric lights were invented, artists often designed complicated shades to cover their huge studio windows to control the light source. And the mystical "north light" coming from towering windows was the only source for work light. Today we can take advantage of scientifically produced fluorescent lights that come very close to imitating natural light, enabling us to work well into late evening and for a full day during the short days of winter.

LIGHTING THE MODEL

In lighting the model, you must first decide if you want to paint the subject from the shadow side or the light side. Figure 27 shows more of the subject's face in shadow, and Figure 28 shows more of the face in light. Some artists feel that painting a man's portrait from the shadow side brings out the character and modeling of the face, and that a woman's portrait is bet-

26. PLACEMENT OF THE SUBJECT
(opposite page)
Here are four photographs of a painting showing four different ways I could have cropped the same subject. (A) This is the picture exactly as I painted it. Each of the other versions illustrates an error in composition: (B) The head is too close to the upper edge. (C) Portions of the hands have been cut off. It is almost always wrong to do this, though you'd be surprised at how often beginners do it! (D) The figure is obviously too far to one side.

A

B

C

D

27. LIGHTING: THE LIGHT SIDE
The side of the face turned toward us is in light. The only darks are the cast shadows from the features, and a touch of form shadow along the far side of the face.

28. LIGHTING: THE SHADOW SIDE
The side of the face turned toward us is in shadow. This lighting is stronger and emphasizes the form.

29. PHOTO 1 (above)
Here the light is from the side, with one half the head in light and half in shade.

30. PHOTO 2 (above right)
The main light has moved to the right, and an inverted triangle of light has been created below the eye on our right. This is the beginning of the most desirable lighting.

ter when done from the light side because the values are closer and the forms softer and more subtle—and therefore more feminine. Of course, exceptions to these "rules" are often effective, so be sure to experiment.

POSITIONING THE LIGHT

The position of the main light source in relation to the sitter will have a very important effect on the portrait. I find that having electric lights on rolling stands (described in the chapter on photographic equipment) simplifies the task of moving the lights.

To determine the best lighting for each sitter requires experimentation. Try lighting the head from both sides. Also raise and lower the main light, observing what happens to the shapes of the shadows around the forms of the face as the light is moved. The intensely lit photographs of the Lincoln statue (Figure 29 to 32) show the effects of several different positionings of the main light source.

You can also create different lighting effects through the intensity or strength of the lighting, which will influence the tones on the head. (The wattage of the lamps and bulbs I use is given earlier in the section on photographic equipment.) In a later chapter I'll take you through five different portrait case histories that will include lighting diagrams.

A WORD ABOUT FLATTERY

It is widely assumed by laymen, and even by artists who do not paint portraits, that the portrait painter is engaged constantly in "flattering" his subjects, and I am often asked about this. If I gather that the questioner is implying that the portraitist routinely reports facts that are not true, or perhaps only partly true, I try to resoundingly put the record straight: false flattery has absolutely no part in portrait painting. On the other hand, the portraitist's mission is to portray the subject *at his or her best*—to explore, discover, and report those qualities about the subject that are interesting, informative, and most characteristic. Therefore, although I have never been asked to deliberately flatter or falsify, I always strive to show my subjects at their best.

SUMMARY

By now it should be clear that the total design of the portrait should be a matter of careful and thoughtful consideration. The composition is, of course, partly intellectual. But it is also instinctual and based on your own taste and judgment. Crucial points to watch for are where objects come in contact with each other and where they overlap. Remember, simplicity, naturalness, and discrimination are the watchwords in composition.

31. PHOTO 3 (above left)
Now the light source has moved further toward the center, and the triangle of light below the eye has connected with the light on the chin. When this happens, you have achieved the most effective lighting for bringing out the forms and character of the face.

32. PHOTO 4 (above)
Now the light has moved so close to the center that the forms on the far right side of the head are beginning to catch the light. This position is too far toward center, and the light is too evenly distributed across the face.

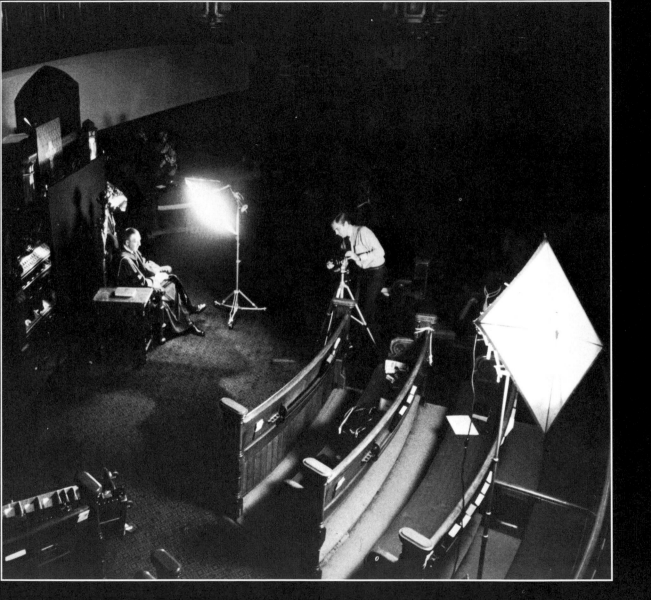

Part III

Executing the Painting

The procedure I have evolved permits sittings to be kept to a minimum despite the painstaking thoroughness of the execution and the successful collaboration of the three individuals involved: artist, client, and subject. The planning meeting takes an hour; the first sitting takes 90 minutes; the second sitting—which is optional—takes an hour; the third sitting, two hours, and the final sitting requires another hour. The total time involved thus demands only six and a half hours of the sitter's time.

When the pressure of a sitter's particularly busy schedule demands it, an even shorter procedure—involving only four and a half hours—is possible. This shorter procedure calls for only three sittings: a photographic session of 90 minutes; an oil-color study, which takes two hours; and the final session of an hour, during which the completed and framed painting is presented to sitter and client for finishing touches, either at my studio or where the painting will be hung.

5

Step-by-Step Procedure

Although painting a portrait actually takes many hours of studio work, I keep the time in which the sitter is physically involved to a minimum. Most people who have achieved enough success in life to be immortalized in a portrait are extremely time-conscious, and I like my subjects to know from the beginning that the portrait will not involve hours and hours of *their* time, only mine.

I personally feel that it is a mistake to perpetuate the myth that good portraits are painted entirely from life, with no photographic assistance. Many artists feel they must apologize for this and hide the fact that they take advantage of photography. However, I have never yet met a portrait subject, other than a professional model who is paid by the hour, who wishes to sit longer than absolutely necessary. Therefore I spend much of the time at sittings sketching and taking photographs of my subject.

One of my most prestigious recent sitters, upon leaving the model stand after about an hour and fifteen minutes, told me that it was the longest time he had sat still in one place during the past ten years! If more potential subjects realized that it was possible to have a good portrait with limited time spent by themselves, I believe a lot more artists would be a lot busier!

THE FIRST SITTING

The first sitting is a photographic session in the subject's home or office, using portable lighting equipment (Figure 33). This modern procedure permits easy experimentation with pose, lighting, costume, accessories, and expression. Working with a camera instead of pencil or oils therefore allows me to be free to record a wide variety of poses in a short time.

I spend at least an hour or two before the scheduled hour of the sitting setting up my lights and using a stand-in to show me exactly what I'm working toward. Then when my sitter arrives I am free to be creative with the pose and concentrate on the composition without being overly concerned with technical aspects of photography. The lighting, however, is of the utmost importance, and I feel that it can make or break a portrait. The first sitting lasts about 90 minutes.

THE SECOND SITTING

If time permits, I like to have a second sitting, which generally lasts about an hour. The second sitting involves more photography. The chosen pose is photographed once more, as I strive to improve the composition, lighting, and expression in my attempts to perfect the pose. For example, I may need to work on the position of a hand or to direct a slight change of stat-

33. A PHOTOGRAPHIC SITTING (overleaf)

At my first sitting with Dr. Bryant M. Kirkland at The Fifth Avenue Presbyterian Church in New York, Elizabeth and I arrived at 8 AM in the sanctuary to set up the lights. My main light, a "Soff-Box," is next to Dr. Kirkland, on his left. My fill-in light, to keep the shadows from going too dark, may be seen in the foreground. I also used a small accent light behind the screen to Dr. Kirkland's left. I use my Koni-Omega 120-mm camera at a distance far enough to avoid camera distortion. (See Chapter 2 for further details on photographic procedure and Chapter 7 for more on my sittings with Dr. Kirkland.)

**34. THE OIL COLOR HEAD STUDY—
ON LOCATION**
*Here I'm working on the oil head study of Dr.
Bryant Kirkland in the church building. This
third-floor room has a stage with huge north
windows. While it served as an excellent studio, I still needed my electric lights to intens-
ify and focus the lighting on the subject.*

ure. I also find that my sitter is more relaxed the second time around, and
so I am usually able to achieve a more natural expression and posture with
the aid of my camera.

THE THIRD SITTING
After I have edited the photographic proofs to some degree and have selected two or three poses I find promising, I usually review the proofs with
my client. I want to retain control over this part of the job, but I also want
the client's reaction to the photographs. (If I am on location, I try to find a
custom laboratory that can process my film and print contact proofs over-
night.)

Ideally, the third sitting, which lasts about two hours, takes place a
week after the previous sitting, though on location (Figure 34) it usually
occurs on the following day. If possible, I generally prefer this sitting to
take place in my New York studio (Figure 35).

*35. THE OIL COLOR HEAD STUDY—
IN THE STUDIO*
*This sitting (in this case my second) with Mr.
Lewis W. Foy of the Bethlehem Steel Corporation took place in my New York studio. Mr.
Foy was much more relaxed away from the
pressures of the office, where our first sitting
had taken place, and I was able to get to know
him better here and make this careful study
for the final painting.*

During the third sitting, I do a careful oil-color study of my subject, taking care to accurately record hair color, eye color, and complexion color
because, when working on the informal head study, it is the colors, values, and general mood of the sitter that I am after (Figure 36). I will depend
heavily on this sketch when I do my final canvas. *Painting from life is an all-
important step in the procedure I am describing in this chapter, and unless an artist
has extensive experience in this type of premier coup painting, any work done from
reference material will look lifeless and monochromatic.* (I recommend my first
book, *Painting the Head in Oil*, to all artists who need to study painting
directly from the model without reference material. I have already
analyzed in depth the difficulties that must be overcome when working
with reference material in Chapter 2 of this book.)

THE COMPOSITIONAL OR QUARTER-SIZE STUDY

Now, working without the sitter, I'm ready for a really important step: the
compositional or quarter-size study. I usually paint this small oil study on
a sheet of Strathmore drawing paper (one-ply, cold-pressed surface) at
half the dimensions of the final painting. In other words, a 40 x 30" (102 x
76 cm) canvas would call for a quarter-size study of 20 x 15" (51 x 38 cm).

36. MR. WALTER J. MATTHEWS
Oil on canvas, 24 x 20" (61 x 51 cm). Here is an oil color head study done as part of the preparation for a business portrait. All of the important information was captured here during a sitting that lasted about two hours.

Thus any measurement in the study is exactly doubled in the final painting, and the study itself would fit into one quarter of the final painting surface.

I do my designing in the quarter-size study—selectively choosing elements from the photographic reference material, then work out the color scheme and the value and tonal plan of the final painting. (Figure 37). In other words, the color and tone of the background and its relationship to the hair and costume colors and the sitter's complexion established during the sittings may be altered at this point for a more pleasing effect.

I also choose the background color now. In choosing a suitable color, I find that light backgrounds project an upbeat, optimistic attitude and give the portrait an instantly recognized contemporary look. Dark backgrounds, on the other hand, can be used for strength and a dramatic effect.

There are two reasons for doing this compositional study. First, as I explained, it gives me the opportunity to work out the composition of the painting to my own satisfaction. And since it's much easier to make changes and adjustments here than on the large canvas, a good study enables me to attack the final canvas premier coup, without hesitation. The second reason is that I can mat this study and show it to my client so he can see how I intend to paint the final canvas and can offer suggestions and criticisms if he wishes. Thus the client will be able to visualize the final canvas along with me and won't be caught by surprise when the final version is unveiled. But if you intend to show this quarter-size study to your client, one word of advice: don't even attempt to suggest the features of your subject. Just leave the face a blank flesh tone. Because unless you

*37. THE COMPOSITIONAL
OR QUARTER-SIZE STUDY
Here I'm working out the final details of color
and composition on a small study for the portrait of the Alafin of Oyo, Nigeria (see Chapter 7 for more about this commission). As you
can see, I have surrounded myself with various reference material. Since the final canvas
was quite large—it was to measure 92 x 60"
(234 x 152 cm)—I painted the study about half
the size of my normal quarter-size study. (In
other words, one eighth the size of the final
painting.) I also put more detail in the face
than is usually advisable.*

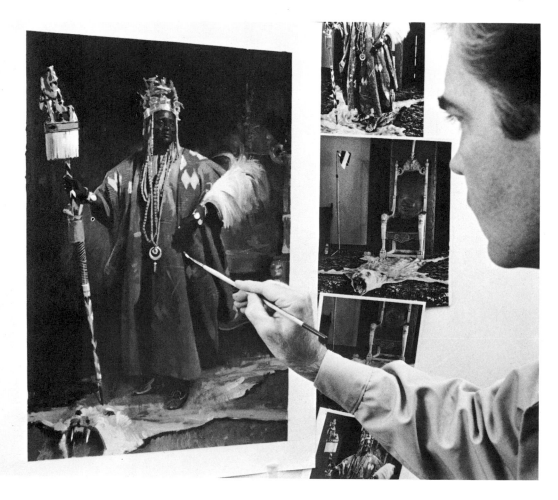

take the time to make it *perfect*—and that is not the point of this step—all your client will see is that "the nose is too long" or "the mouth is wrong," and he will be unable to evaluate the composition as a whole. The result will be that instead of being reassured about the final version, he will end up worrying about it.

THE FINAL CANVAS
Once I have worked out all the details of design and color in my small study, I am ready to work on the final painting.

The first step with the large canvas is to make a very meticulous drawing of my subject and the setting in which I have decided to place him. I use a soft number 2 pencil for this step, which allows corrections to be made easily, and when I am satisfied with the drawing, I use Blair fixative to insure that the pencil marks will not smudge into the paint.

Then, at last, I am ready to work on the painting itself. This is usually the most enjoyable part of a long process, and I always free my calendar from early morning to late at night for a week or two of continuous, uninterrupted studio time. I spend from 40 to 80 hours on each final canvas, depending on the complexity. (Details of the painting technique will be described later in Chapter 7.)

THE FINAL SITTING
The final sitting gives me the opportunity to check the painting against the subject and make any necessary adjustments or alterations. Sometimes the eye color is not quite right, or something in the expression is not

38. A FINAL SITTING
The final sitting for Mr. Walter Connolly took place in my New York studio. I worked with Mr. Connolly for about an hour until Mrs. Connolly arrived. Then the final version was revealed and they were both quite pleased. We made plans to personally deliver the painting to Hartford the following week so that we could participate in the selection of the spot where the painting would hang. I don't often attend unveiling ceremonies, but this was to be only a small group and the painting had been so well received that we decided to go. I took along my French easel in case further touch-ups were requested, but they were not needed.

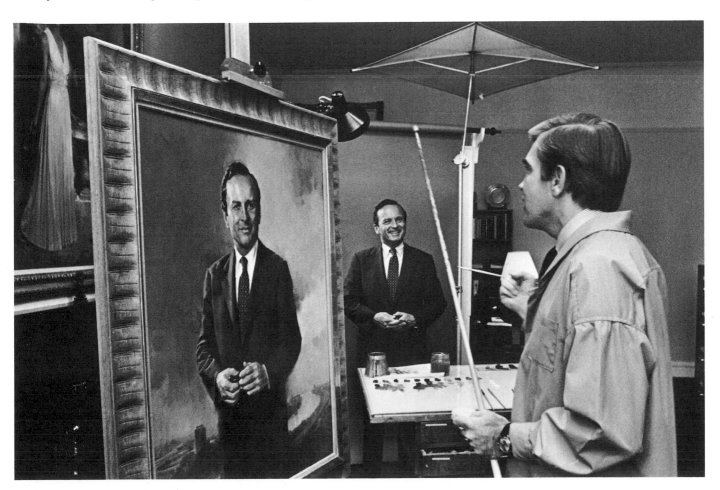

exactly as it should be and a touch or two will make it right.

For the final sitting, I usually schedule the sitter to be present so I can accomplish at least an hour of careful work before the client, or in some cases the spouse of the subject, arrives to comment (Figure 39). I always let the sitter and other visitors who come to the studio feel free to comment on the portrait. I try to undertake any corrections they might suggest, as long as they are within reason, since I want both my subject and the client to be pleased with the final work. They also enjoy having the opportunity to work with me at this final stage. But if a major change is requested— such as changing the position of a hand, or adding something to the background, I arrange for an additional sitting so I may have ample time to work on it.

When the final version is revealed for the first time, the moment is electric with emotion. I try to watch the faces of my clients to get their reactions. In most cases the experience is a happy one all the way around and final plans are made for delivery of the portrait. My gallery handles this step.

A WORD ON WORKING WITH CLIENTS

Always remember that the purpose of a commissioned portrait—quite apart from your own satisfaction—is to give pleasure to the person who commissioned it. If it does not produce pleasure, the artist has failed in his purpose. This doesn't mean that you have to sacrifice your artistic integrity. Far from it! When I have completed a painting that I feel really good about, that really excites me, and it has never failed that my client is also pleased. When I feel less sure of a painting, it does not seem to get as good a response from the client. So I paint for myself first of all. And I find that if I make a hit by my own standards, my client is enthusiastic too.

Don't be afraid of taking suggestions from your clients. They will be looking at the portrait from an entirely different point of view from yours, and it is valuable input. You must give them the opportunity to offer suggestions, and then you must evaluate these suggestions and decide how to proceed. The lay person, untrained in artistic matters, may not be able to specifically point to the problem that is troubling him, but his suggestions may make you more sensitive and aware of an area that needs work.

Very often, at the final sitting, I am able to make a stroke or two, here and there on the canvas, at the client's prompting that will add immeasurably to his enjoyment of the painting. This certainly doesn't compromise my integrity. Quite the opposite, I take pride in this part of my professional responsibility to my client.

PHOTOGRAPHING THE FINISHED PAINTING

After the painting is finished, it is advisable to have slides or prints made of your work for your records. After the client approves the finished painting, my photographer picks it up, makes a color print of it, and keeps the negative on file for future copies if I need them. (I record the photographer's copy negative number of the print at the bottom of the "Commission Details" form (Figure 42) in case I ever need to make duplicates.)

Five Case Histories

6

The one lesson I hope to convey in this book is the value of careful pre-planning. I believe with all my heart that thoughtful, creative, preliminary study and planning followed by conscientious attention to detail in the final execution is the path to a successful portrait! In this chapter I will show you some of the sketches and studies that led to the solution of several assignments.

CASE 1. HIS MAJESTY THE ALAFIN OF OYO

I will always remember this portrait assignment as one of the most unique and interesting of my career. After I completed the double portrait of Chief A. Oladeinde Fernandez and his wife (page 102), Chief Fernandez invited Elizabeth and me to Nigeria to work on portraits of kings of the great Yoruba people.

The portrait painter does not receive many commissions for full-length state portraits of reigning monarchs. In this case, the subject of the painting was the distinguished occupant of a throne with a lineage going back many centuries into the ancient history of Africa. I therefore approached this assignment in an attitude of genuine awe and strove to produce a painting that would capture the young ruler's dignity, elegance, and historic aura.

In May of 1977, we left Washington, D.C., via the Concorde jet to London and then went on to Lagos, Nigeria. There we were met by a team of Africans who were to be our guides and assistants throughout our visit. We were taken by jeep 135 miles north to the city of Oyo, the site of the throne of the Alafin (King) of Oyo, who occupies one of the most historic thrones of the Yoruba tribe.

On that day Elizabeth and I met the Alafin for the first time in his audience chamber. While his men prostrated themselves before him, we removed our shoes, as their custom required, ascended the steps to his throne, and were seated on either side of him. We briefly discussed his portrait during this first meeting.

Our sittings took place the next day in a large room with tall Palladian windows that worked well as a studio. I used my Koni-Omega camera and, with my studio lights hooked up to current transformers, recorded the Alafin in the formal costume he wished to wear in the portrait.

The following day, I painted a sketch. Because of the extreme heat, we worked informally and the Alafin was dressed casually. After three days of hard work, we returned to Lagos. In London I had my film developed. I had taken two hundred photos of the Alafin.

Upon our return to New York, I assembled my reference material and worked for several months on the 92 x 60″ (234 x 152 cm) canvas. The final painting was framed, crated, and shipped to Nigeria the following summer.

POSING WITH THE ALAFIN
After the work was complete, one of our aides took this photograph.

AT WORK ON THE HEAD STUDY AT THE PALACE IN OYO
I draped Elizabeth's white sweater over the back of the throne to provide a light background for the sketch.

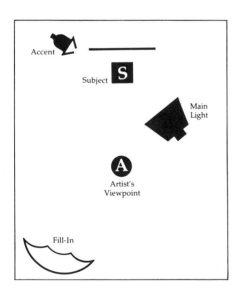

LIGHTING DIAGRAM
The main light source is to the right of center. The small accent light comes from the left, adding a crisp definition to the side edges of the figure and the scepter. In taking the photographs, the white umbrella I used to reflect the fill-in light was placed well away from the shadow side.

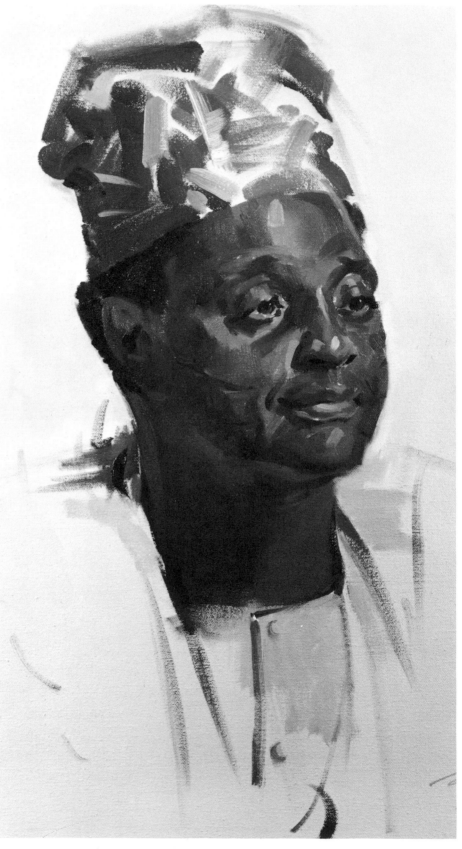

DETAIL OF THE HEAD STUDY
I painted the head study of the Alafin of Oyo while he posed in informal clothing.

COMPOSITIONAL STUDY

This small study, 25 x 16" (64 x 41 cm) was painted in oil on one-ply, cold pressed Strathmore drawing paper. It was done as a preliminary study for the finished painting which appears on the following page. The compositional study serves two principal functions. First, it allows me to plan my composition on a small scale and gives me the chance to work out problems involving color, tone, and arrangement. Secondly, I can show this study to my client (I almost always do) to give him a good idea of what the final painting will be like. I am careful to not include too much detail, however. At this point detail would only be disturbing and distract from the compositional purpose of this sketch.

76

HIS MAJESTY THE ALAFIN OF OYO (left)
Oil on canvas, 92 x 60" (234 x 152 cm), collection Chief A. Oladeinde Fernandez, Lagos, Nigeria. The young Nigerian king wears a robe embroidered with gold and holds a beaded sceptre and an oxtail fan. On his head is the ancient crown of Oyo.

DETAIL OF THE HEAD (above)
This close-up detail of the final painting shows the dignity of the young king's expression. The scars on his face were extremely important, as they denote not only his tribe but the fact that he is a king. He was very concerned that I render them exactly right.

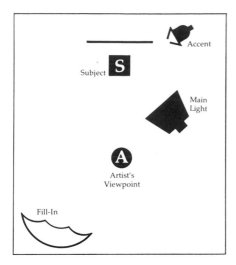

CASE 2. DR. BRYANT M. KIRKLAND

This portrait was commissioned by the Fifth Avenue Presbyterian Church of its very distinguished minister, Dr. Bryant M. Kirkland. As a member of the church, I had studied Dr. Kirkland's face in the pulpit for many years before beginning this painting, and it was a portrait I was very anxious to do.

Our first sitting took place in the main sanctuary of this beautiful and historic church. We brought a large carved chair down from the pulpit and decided after some experimentation that a seated pose would be the best. Dr. Kirkland seemed more relaxed after we had worked for a while and the pose became more natural. My lights had to be placed between the pews, but I was able to achieve a good balance.

On the third floor of the church building, where a stage with huge north windows served as a studio, I painted a study of Dr. Kirkland. I carried this study further than I do some of these studies, and it is really more finished than is necessary in this step. Again, I was mostly interested in recording complexion, eye color, and hair color in this sketch.

I took the large canvas to my summer studio in Connecticut, where I worked on it until it was nearly complete. When I returned to New York, Dr. Kirkland came to my studio for a final sitting.

HEAD STUDY (right)
The head study sketches are a vital step in the process of building a portrait. Later, when the final canvas is complete, I often find these preliminaries too sketchy and inconclusive. But when I am studying the terrain of the subject's face and character with intensity, they give me the information on the head I need to complete my final portrait.

COMPOSITIONAL STUDY

I usually work for about two hours on a study like this, making changes freely. Experimenting here is far easier than in the final version. Leaving the face just a vague blur, as I have done here, allows you (and your client) to focus on the essential problems of design. Here you can see that I intended to include a suggestion of the ornate paneling behind the chair. In the final painting, this was eliminated in favor of a simple dark color.

DR. BRYANT M. KIRKLAND (above)
Oil on canvas, 50 x 45" (127 x 114 cm), collection The Fifth Avenue Presbyterian Church. The Fifth Avenue Presbyterian Church is one of the great churches of New York, and I tried to suggest its historic quality by the inclusion of the original pulpit chair in this portrait of Fifth Avenue's famed senior minister. Perhaps the overall effect of the painting is darker than it should be, but I felt that the strong colors of the robe and hood would be sufficient to keep the composition vital. Of course, the intense and inescapable gaze of Dr. Kirkland is the principal feature. This is one of those portraits where the eyes follow you wherever you move in the room where the portrait is hung—a quality considered very remarkable by the public. Artists, of course, know that to achieve this mysterious quality, all you must do is ask the sitter to look directly at you while you paint.

DETAIL OF THE HEAD (right)
To create a feeling of three-dimensional depth, most portrait heads are painted so that the background is darker on the light side of the face and lighter on the dark side. Here is an example where the background is darker on both sides. The main difficulty in achieving the illusion of depth occurs here when the background is darker than the shadow on the face. To solve this problem, I introduced a strong cool highlight on the chair back to contrast with the dark of the hair and help soften the silhouette just behind the ear on the right. The direct full-face portrait poses special problems also: It is the most difficult pose to draw, it does not express form as fully as the three-quarter view, and it requires that the artist master the difficulties of an almost symmetrical shape. But I chose the full-face view because this was the only view that could communicate the full impression of the candor and authority of this distinguished clergyman.

CASE 3. MR. WALTER J. CONNOLLY, JR.

Mr. Walter Connolly, of the Connecticut Bank and Trust Company in Hartford, was an enthusiastic subject and a pleasure to paint. Our first meeting took place at our 1979 National Portrait Seminar, when Mr. Connolly stopped by the Barbizon Plaza Hotel to say hello. I remember that I was impressed by his vigor and animation and was eager to portray him.

Our first sittings took place at the bank in Hartford, where I worked on the top floor of the building. The view was magnificent. We worked on a variety of poses, but decided on a standing pose with the city seen from the window as a background. A few weeks later, Mr. Connolly came to New York, where we worked on the color sketches and took additional photographs.

This was a painting that moved along well from the very first stroke. There are some portraits that go more smoothly than others, and all conditions must have been just right. I barely remember painting it. The painting just almost happened by itself.

Our final sitting took place in New York, but I took the painting myself to Hartford to help hang it. I also brought along my French easel and paints, but no further work was necessary.

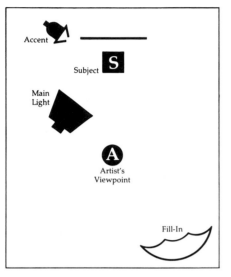

LIGHTING DIAGRAM (above)
Here the main light is to our left, as is the accent light. I often use an accent light because it adds sparkle and interest and brings out the form. But a single main light source is easier to paint and until you have a lot of experience, it is better to use only one light source.

HEAD STUDY (right)
In this case, I knew just the pose I wanted to use for Mr. Connolly's portrait: smiling and looking up and to the right. I placed an accent light offstage to the left, and put the main light source rather high and to the left of center. Mr. Connolly has a healthy, friendly, animated manner and I tried to capture it in the sketch. I had to remind myself, however, that the main purpose of this stage is to record precise details of color.

COMPOSITIONAL STUDY

Preliminary studies can be painted directly from life or from reference material. Regardless of the source, the compositional study is an important step. In the preliminary study, the entire composition is placed before you in simplified form. Since changes can readily be made without difficulty now, I usually make my experimental changes directly on the sketch, wiping them off later if I don't like the effect. Sometimes I make changes (including those suggested by my client) on an acetate overlay. I then can place the change over the painting and preview its effect before I actually change the painting. If you are having trouble deciding the size of the final canvas, you can put the compositional study to valuable use. Shoot a slide of the study and project it on the wall— even the actual wall where the painting will hang, if it is conveniently nearby. By varying the size of the projected image, you can decide the size of the final portrait accordingly.

MR. WALTER J. CONNOLLY, JR. (left)
Oil on canvas, 44 x 36" (112 x 91 cm), collection Connecticut Bank and Trust Company, Hartford. The large size which I was permitted to make this painting allowed me the spacious effect I like in a portrait. The pose—front-facing, erect, and commanding—is ideal for an official business portrait that is to hang in a public place. Mr. Connolly's hands fell naturally into a handsome relationship. A word of advice to the beginning portraitist: in an official painting, which is to hang in a collection of previously completed portraits, be sure that your image size is large enough. Often you must use a ten-inch head to achieve the strength that is needed, even if this goes somewhat over actual life size.

DETAIL OF THE HEAD (above)
As you can see, the head in the final painting is carried much further than the study and a great many refinements are made. The general complexion is also slightly cooler. One of the pleasures of using outdoor backgrounds such as in this painting is that I'm able to incorporate strong blue and green reflected lights all around the head, as I would if the sitter were actually posing outdoors.

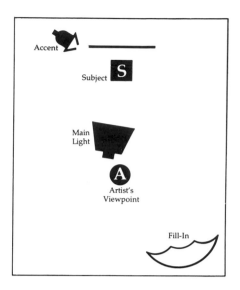

LIGHTING DIAGRAM (above)
Here the main light source is almost directly behind me and just slightly to the left. The cast shadow beneath the sitter's nose reveals the exact location of the main light. This creates a broad overall lighting effect that is very soft and attractive to paint. The accent light illuminates the edge of the hair and forehead.

CASE 4. MRS. RICHARD KLARBERG

This portrait assignment, which was commissioned by Mrs. Klarberg's parents, was difficult because there were so many possibilities from which to choose. Emily Klarberg looked so lovely in every outfit she suggested that I wish I had painted several versions of her. At one point we almost went off to Central Park to work outdoors in casual clothes, with her dog to be included. Finally, after much deliberation, I painted the compositional sketch, which I showed to Mr. and Mrs. Gawthrop, and the matter was settled.

Since Mrs. Klarberg lives in New York, it was easy for her to come to my studio, and we worked there on several occasions.

Before she arrived, I had fresh flowers sent in so I could arrange a colorful background against her black dress. I particularly liked the design on the front and sleeves of the dress and found it a good complement to the flowers in the background.

HEAD STUDY (right)
I normally work about two hours on this study. Its purpose is to record hair color, general facial coloring, iris color, and lip color, and I am especially careful to get these facts correct. Then I go on to record as many other details of interest as I can. Here the sitter's high coloring was especially attractive. This sketch was painted from a different angle than the final painting and we had not yet decided to sweep the hair back away from the face.

MRS. RICHARD KLARBERG
Oil on canvas, 36 x 30" (91 x 76 cm), collection Mr. and Mrs. Klarberg. The black dress with its white braiding was so striking that I wanted to show it off well. I selected a frank, straightforward gaze as the basis of the composition and gave her hands a prominent position. The background is painted mainly in washes of thin color with the flowers indicated casually with somewhat more opaque color. The head was set off by warm, opaque scumbles at the top of the canvas. The tonal plan, with all four corners the same value, is unusual in my work, but I liked the effect and I plan to use this scheme again.

CASE 5. MR. ROBERT S. SCHEU

When this portrait of Mr. Scheu was commissioned by his bank in Buffalo, he had already taken early retirement and was enjoying an adventurous life on his sailboat. He came to New York for the sittings, and we immediately decided to depart from a formal business setting and portray him in a much more casual mood than is often found in business portraits. Mr. Scheu was seated in the studio on the edge of the model stand, which was turned into a stone parapet in the painting. The boat added to the background was copied from a family snapshot. To give an outdoors effect to the lighting on Mr. Scheu, I used basically the same lighting plan as is shown for Mr. Connolly, but I added an overhead umbrella light placed on a boom, to create a soft, downlit effect.

COMPOSITIONAL STUDY (above)
As I have stated many times before, the main purpose of the compositional study is to plan your overall arrangement, your tones, and your colors. It is therefore wise to omit all detail, at this stage, particularly in the face. In this case, however, the slight suggestion of features helped me to see that the turn of the head in the final painting would be preferable.

HEAD STUDY (right)
This study shows how abbreviated this step can be and still record the essential material: eye color, hair color, and complexion color. I enjoyed an animated conversation with Mr. Scheu as we worked and felt it unnecessary to record more visual information than is shown here because the sketch told me the essentials of coloring and had a spirit that additional work would not enhance.

MR. ROBERT S. SCHEU
Oil on canvas, 38 x 32" (96 x 81 cm), collection Marine Midland Bank, Buffalo. By comparing this final painting to the study, you can see the slightly changed pose, with the head turned to our left. I liked the flow of the composition better here and I think it is a more flattering view of the subject, too.

7 Painting Technique

I would like to recommend to you the so-called premier coup technique for the execution of your portraits. It is an extremely difficult and demanding technique, but one that is full of excitement and possibilities. It may not suit you, but at least try it as I will describe it in this chapter. Your technique eventually will be a very personal thing, arrived at after you have experimented with various procedures.

The term *premier coup* translated from the French means "at first blow." Thus the premier coup technique implies the execution of the painting as a single, direct passage of paint, bringing the forms of the composition to as full a realization as possible in the initial effort. Of course, this requires thorough planning and careful preparation. You cannot approach the final canvas with hesitation. The doubts and alternatives must be cleared away in the preliminary studies, allowing the final execution to go forward with boldness and decisiveness.

With your preliminary studies complete, as described in Chapters 3 and 4, your procedure is as follows:

PRELIMINARY PREPARATION

Carefully arrange the "field of battle" the evening or afternoon before you will begin the canvas. Your white, stretched canvas is on the easel with its carefully executed drawing. The quarter-size study is on a nearby easel, as is your life study of the head. Your brushes, mediums, and all other tools and supplies are ready and arranged for action.

You may or may not decide to have the sitter present. This is up to you. I usually prefer to work alone at this point. My concentration and effort are so intense that the sitter would actually be a distraction. I have made an intense study of the subject, and now I intend to concentrate my efforts. Conversation, movement, and variation would only distract me from what I want to do.

The morning the painting session is to begin I rise early, have a good breakfast, and try to dispatch the morning routine quickly and smoothly. I plan to be in the studio early (about 7:00 AM) with my mind at ease and free of clutter. This is very important. The studio is in perfect order and everything except the job at hand has been put away. There are no distractions.

Most important of all, I have no appointments for the day and, if I can arrange it, none in the evening. I try to have *nothing* on my mind except the painting. Sometimes a little background music from the radio is helpful as an aid to concentration, but that is all.

MIXING THE PRINCIPAL COLORS

I begin usually with the background or the garments—the largest shapes. My first step is to set the quarter-size study on its easel right next to the palette. Now I carefully prepare eight or ten piles of paint for the principal colors of the area I intend to complete that day.

The preparation of these color batches is a critical procedural step and merits our attention. The purpose is to prepare sufficient quantities of needed colors so that the execution can proceed unimpeded and directly, with generous amounts of pigment on hand. A second purpose is that by preparing sizable quantities of the colors that will form the basis of my picture I will be able to store them for further work and/or improvements.

For each major form or element in the painting I prepare at least five batches of color: a darkest dark, a dark halftone, a middle tone, a light halftone, and a light. (If I am painting a businessman's gray suit, the local color—gray—is the tone he thinks of when he visualizes his "gray suit." Only the artist sees the many other tones in the suit.) It may be that the middle tone, in the case of a garment, will be the local color of that garment in normal studio light. Then it is that middle tone that must be adjusted most carefully.

If I also plan to paint the background that day, I will mix the main tones for the background too. I actually touch the mixtures of paint to the surface of the quarter-size study to make sure I am matching them precisely.

These large piles of basic tones are then "orchestrated" by making many variations of them as I work. Of course, I always have my full pal-

39. EXECUTING THE PORTRAIT
As I paint, I surround myself with the small sketch, the head study, and other reference material.

91

TWO FIGURES
Oil on canvas, 70 x 54" (178 x 137 cm), collection the artist. You must be conscious, above all, of the edges in your painting. Keep them soft and flowing. Let the tones and colors flow and merge together. Harsh, sharp edges are trouble sources.

DETAIL OF TWO FIGURES
(opposite page)
Nothing is quite so important as achieving a "flowing" character in the brushwork, making the various forms and areas of the painting flow and merge into each other. Here, the dark background shape flows through several intermediate tones into left shoulder. The dark of the hair flows into the shadow of the hat. The hair and dress flow together. Throughout the painting, almost all of the edges are soft. Where they are not soft, such as on the hat brim, the contrast is startling and provides an eye-catching accent. Certain subjects lend themselves to this flowing technique: a woman's softly curling hair, gentle folds in a dress, draperies—all objects I love to paint.

ette set out as I work, and I am constantly dipping into the various standard colors on my palette to create interesting variations to the basic tones that I have prepared for the day's work.

PLANNING THE DAY'S WORK

This brings me to an important point: each day's work on the canvas should be planned. You may find, as I do, that an entire day will be required for the garments alone. The background may require an entire day. Of course, the head will need a full day's work, at least. The hands will require their own day. Special details in the painting, such as props or jewelry, may require a day. The artist must orchestrate and plan the execution so that contiguous passages are freshly wet as they meet, enabling the paint to be blended or merged, as desired.

All in all, the execution of a complex subject in the premier coup technique requires a high degree of overseeing and organization to accomplish it effectively. After you have worked this way for a while, though, you will probably find that planning your painting's execution is no more complicated than planning a meal of several courses.

STORING THE PAINT

There are several possibilities for storing the piles of paint from day to day or session to session. Perhaps the most effective is to add a drop or two of clove oil to each batch of paint to retard the drying. Another possibility is to transfer the batches from the palette to strips of glass and immerse them in a tray of water. Some artists even store the paint in the refrigerator.

ADVANTAGES OF A PREMIER COUP TECHNIQUE

All this may seem like a lot of trouble, but there are two tremendous benefits. First, a premier coup painting—one passage of paint kept wet until complete, with only minor additions later—is the *most permanent* oil technique. Secondly, there is no other approach that will permit you the *freedom* and that will give you the *immediacy* that is so vital in portraiture.

TECHNICAL ADVICE

As I begin to paint, I observe the time-honored painting traditions, such as keeping the darks relatively thin and building up the lights opaquely. Of course, I begin each section of the painting with the darks, moving on to the halftones, and ending with the lights. I also try to use the largest brush I can to do any given job, striving for a flowing, loose, broad brush technique.

I will now show you several of my paintings and tell you how I approached particular problems in each one.

MR. BEN HERMAN
Oil on canvas, 36 x 30" (91 x 76 cm).

*Simplify the forms in the hand.
Eliminate unnecessary detail.*

*Brush the edges of form and back-
ground together.*

*Consider each brushstroke before
you make it. The strokes here flow
crisply with the form of the folds
and wrinkles.*

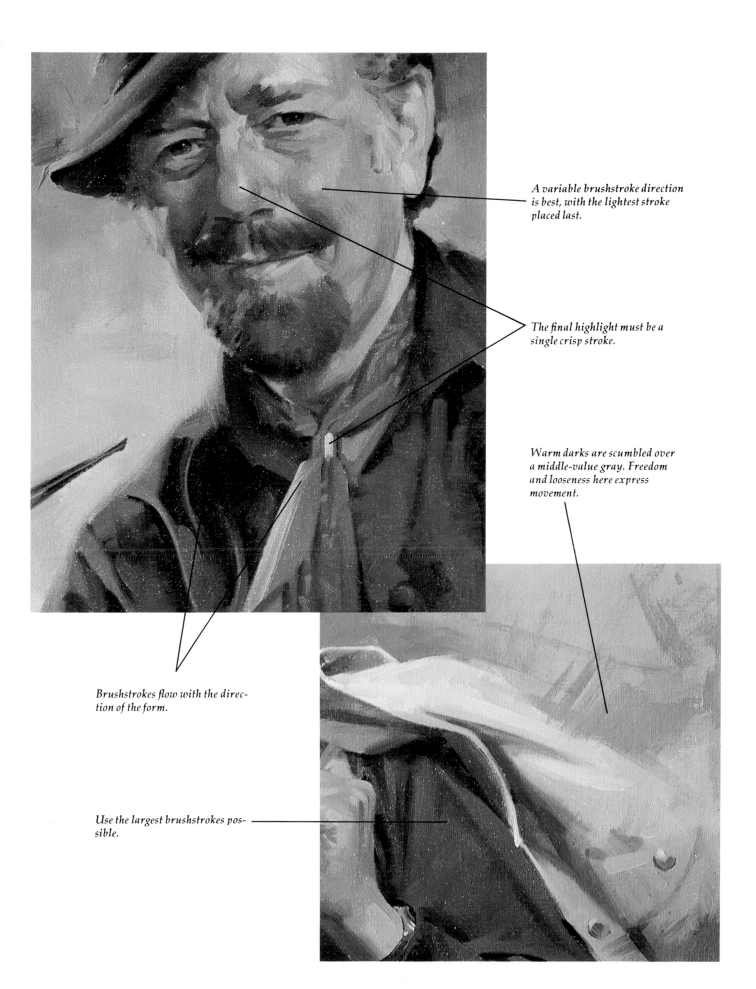

A variable brushstroke direction is best, with the lightest stroke placed last.

The final highlight must be a single crisp stroke.

Warm darks are scumbled over a middle-value gray. Freedom and looseness here express movement.

Brushstrokes flow with the direction of the form.

Use the largest brushstrokes possible.

PORTRAIT OF CHRIST *(left)*
Oil on canvas, 70 x 54" (178 x 137 cm), collection The Fifth Avenue Presbyterian Church, New York. This is a large canvas, and the vast openness of the background was painted entirely with huge bristle flats. I wanted to achieve a feeling of spaciousness and freedom, and the loose brushwork helped. It was a great amount of painting surface to "keep going" at once, but the oil of cloves in my paint allowed me to "fuse" the tones of the background together, and then to blend the tones of the robe into the background. Except for minor accents in the garment and face, there are no hard edges in this picture.

DETAIL OF THE BRUSHWORK *(above)*
I felt great freedom while painting this head, partly because I was painting an idea in my mind, an inspiration if you will, rather than an objective record of a set of visual facts, hence the freedom of brushwork which you see here. It is always important to me to see that the head and background are successfully merged. Hard edges here would have spoiled the effect. In painting the face, I strive for variety in the direction and emphasis of the brushstrokes. The shadows here are painted very thinly, while the lights are rich and opaque.

DETAIL OF THE HEAD

The strong accent light striking the left side of the subject's head is painted with a mixture of white, cadmium orange, and a touch of alizarin crimson. The reflected light on the right side of the head has chromium oxide green as its basis. I suppose there is no more difficult passage in a portrait than the meeting of hair and forehead. Here the flesh tones and hair tones must be intermingled to achieve a natural as well as realistic effect. Throughout the forms of the face, brushstroke direction is important, the strokes generally moving "with the form" (that is, following the form's general contour) to add to the illusion of depth.

DETAIL OF THE HANDS

Two competing objectives are usually involved when painting hands in a portrait. One is the desire to paint a simplified, elegant hand with minimal detail. The other is to introduce sufficient detail to achieve strength and character. Only your own preference and experience can tell you how to proceed between the push-pull of these opposing goals. In this hand, the lights and darks are warm and the halftones cool. The line formed by the index finger pressing against the book is probably the hardest edge in the entire painting. The darks of the hand merge into the darks of the book and robe.

DR. JOSEPH DiPALMA
Oil on canvas, 42 x 34" (107 x 86 cm), collection The Hahnemann Medical College and Hospital of Philadelphia. Introducing some intense warm colors into the darkest darks of the garments relieves the deadness of a heavy passage. I added strokes of intense alizarin and burnt sienna in the deep folds of robe. The facing of the robe is velvet. The highlights on velvet are always a little more "contrasty" than those on more conventional fabric, and the folds are a bit softer. The cool background here is basically all one tone and value, with warm flourishes for contrast.

DETAIL OF THE STAINED GLASS (above)
I took one terrific liberty with reality: the stained glass fragment Mr. Douglass holds actually appeared very dark—almost black. To show that it was, in fact, colored glass, I reversed the light and increased the intensity of the colors many times.

MR. GEORGE DOUGLASS (right)
Oil on canvas, 33 x 36" (84 x 91 cm), collection Mr. and Mrs. George Douglass. This was my first commissioned portrait after moving to New York. I was very conscious of style and brushwork, and there's a strong pattern of brushstrokes that moves horizontally across the composition. The whites and light halftones flow together, and the dark tones hold together.

CHIEF AND MRS. A. OLADEINDE FERNANDEZ
Oil on canvas, 70 x 60" (178 x 152 cm), collection Chief Fernandez. The brilliant colors and intricate detail of these costumes demanded a large unbroken background—it is really just space with a splash of colors throughout it. Yes, a double portrait is a difficult assignment, but a challenging and fascinating one. Here we have the interplay of two magnetic personalities and a profusion of intricate detail in costumes. Quite a lot for one canvas, even a large canvas like this one! The sidelight from the left helps to bring the forms out from the background.

DETAIL OF THE COSTUME

The details of the beads, ceremonial pendants, and symbolic weaving in the robe were all extremely important to the effectiveness of this portrait, and I tried to take extraordinary efforts to complete them accurately. The jewelry was first drawn very carefully: the beads in each row were carefully counted and measured! Then the individual beads were painted one by one, until the job was done. A lot of work, but exciting when it was finished.

MR. LEWIS W. FOY
Oil on canvas, 44 x 36" (112 x 91 cm), collection Bethlehem Steel Corporation. In planning this portrait, I felt that a low-key, cool color scheme would be best, so I played the rich blue of Mr. Foy's suit against another blue. The warm tones in the chair and floor provide contrast and relief. Most of these blue passages were painted quite thinly. The strongly lighted head, suit, tie, and hands were painted in a full-bodied, opaque manner. (Mr. Foy can also be seen posing for the oil study for his portrait on page 68.)

DETAIL OF THE HEAD (above)
In painting a portrait head, the first priority is to achieve a solid, three-dimensional form. Three-dimensionality is expressed through values—by the interplay of light and shade. Between the brilliant lights and the dark tones lie the complex transitional halftones, and these are the tones that must be most carefully studied. They can make or break the painting!

DETAIL OF THE HANDS (left)
Hands are a study in careful, sensitive, painstaking drawing and painting. That's all there is to it. There is no secret formula in painting hands, just hard work. Here are some suggestions to help. For example, avoid extreme darks in the small areas between the fingers. Notice the shadow cast by the thumb and compare this value to the dark of the suit. Look for the warm and cool colors in the hands, and pay careful attention to the edges.

DR. DONALD F. HORNIG *(left)*
Oil on canvas, 48 x 32" (122 x 81 cm), collection Brown University. In painting these ceremonial robes, I used large filberts. I struck in the darks first, then the large halftone masses, then the lights. I avoided all detail in the beginning and stepped back continually to watch the over-all effect. You'll be surprised how little detail you have to add if the basic effect is accurate. Since I abhor a tight look in my portraits, I'm constantly striving to keep the large, dull areas loose and flowing. Here the chair has splashes of green and red with freely brushed edges.

DETAIL OF THE CHAIN *(above)*
My portraits are not wax-work recreations of subjects. The chain and pendant is carefully drawn here, but loose and free in actual execution. (You can see the actual chain in a display case at the university, if you wish.) My purpose was not to duplicate it exactly, but to capture the total effect of the chain as it sparkled in the light. Some of the wet red paint of the robe was actually dragged into the reflected lights of the chain. And the brightest lights glitter to the point where the contour of the chain disappears in the red background. Always remember that you are painting, not copying.

MRS. RICHARD HORN
Oil on canvas, 30 x 27" (76 x 69 cm), collection Mrs. Horn. One of the most exciting and creative ways to develop a painting is to conceive of the entire composition as a "bouquet of colors," subordinating the specific realism to a subjective interpretation and accentuation. Here the small bouquet of flowers becomes the motif. The colors of the flowers are repeated everywhere throughout the painting, even to the point of actually expanding into the air around them. The contours of the dress are particularly soft and the colors of the dress are "set loose" into the background. Of special interest is the abstract-shaped blue accent placed immediately behind the head with a palette knife.

DETAIL OF THE FLOWERS

In a portrait, a floral bouquet like this is of greatest value as an effect. It would be a mistake to render the flowers petal by petal. That is not to say that the flowers should not be realistic. They should—there must be certain details that are precisely right, and that ring true. But the color can flow right out of the contour of the flower to animate the surrounding area. This little arrangement became the motif for the color scheme of the entire painting.

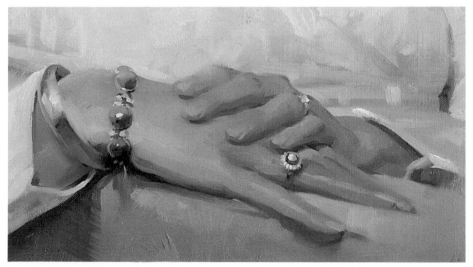

DETAIL OF THE HANDS

The hands of a graceful female subject should be presented with an elegant simplicity. The gesture and arrangement of the hands is first, their color and tone second, and all detail is subordinated. Carefully painted highlights flow down each finger. The nails are just suggested. Here is a very important point: pay close attention to the jewelry. It has probably been carefully selected by your subject and doubtless has intense sentimental value. Respect it, observe it closely, and paint it with care. Make it sparkle!

MR. PETER KIEWIT (opposite page)

Oil on canvas, 48 x 34" (122 x 86 cm), collection Mrs. Peter Kiewit. Posthumous portraits are an important part of the work of any busy portraitist. This painting of a distinguished Omaha, Nebraska, builder and philanthropist is an example. I had a sitting scheduled with Mr. Kiewit in my New York studio, but a riding accident and his subsequent illness and death intervened and I missed the opportunity of getting to know this brilliant and successful man. Excellent professional-quality photographs of him were available, however; the best one is shown at right. This was a particularly good pose, and the studio made handsome color enlargements for me to work from. In addition, Mrs. Kiewit provided me with a generous supply of candid pictures. Snapshots are extremely helpful in supplementing a visual impression when you are unable to be with the sitter. To overcome the tendency to copy the photograph, I set the photograph on an easel where the model would ordinarily stand or sit, and I stood back and tried to paint as vigorously and aggressively as if I were working from life.

DETAIL OF THE COSTUME (below)

The details of the folds are executed as simply and crisply as possible, but not with a slapdash hurry. Every stroke is carefully planned. Objects such as the cufflinks and the pocket handkerchief should be carefully drawn and thoughtfully executed, but not overly detailed. Often a few deft strokes are all that is necessary.

HIS MAJESTY THE ONI OF IFE (left)
Oil on canvas, 70 x 50" (178 x 127 cm), collection Chief A. Oladeinde Fernandez, Lagos, Nigeria. There are several points of technical interest in this rather dramatic portrait of the well-known Nigerian king. The shimmering, reflective quality of the fabric was achieved merely by accentuating the highlights. This always gives a form the sensation of a slight gloss. To relieve the extreme coolness of the large garment, I introduced strong warm reflected lights in most of the darks. This also adds to the mysterious glow of the fabric. This portrait is one in a series of portraits I made of royal Nigerian figures. The dignity, strength, and dramatic visual appeal of these men made them inspiring subjects for portraits.

DETAIL OF THE HEAD (above)
The middle range of tones in the face was painted with a warm mixture of viridian, burnt sienna, and orange. The highlights, as you can see, are extremely cool. They are actually a mixture of ivory black and white. Flickering through the warm tones are touches of chrome green, alizarin crimson, and ultramarine blue. The intricate variety of colors in the painting of a dark-skinned subject is one of the distinctive challenges of painting.

114

DETAIL OF THE HANDS (above)
I hope that this detail shows what I mean by striving for the character and gesture of the hands, eliminating as much detail as possible. Hands are complicated enough, in their intricate drawing, without loading them with detail, as you may see in some portraits. Concentrate on the effect of the hands: what they are doing, and what the light is doing as it strikes them.

MR. ROBERT E. RICH (left)
Oil on canvas, 36 x 30" (91 x 76 cm), collection Rich Products Corporation, Buffalo. The word "scumbling" sounds odd to a layman, but to a painter the term suggests all sorts of ways to enliven a painting. Scumbling involves the reworking of a dried area by dragging a brush of color loosely over it, and perhaps by manipulating the brush in several opposing ways. Near the subject's elbow to the left I scumbled alizarin crimson over the cool background. In fact, there is scumbling everywhere in this painting—mostly warm colors introduced to enrich the cool greens and blues. Not only does scumbling enrich the color, but it also helps to "pull together" an over-blended or fussy passage.

MR. DAVID ROCKEFELLER (above)
Oil on canvas, 20 x 16" (51 x 41 cm). This study was painted in about two hours and the time pressure produced, as it usually does, a result that is stronger in brushwork than the final painting. Here the brushstrokes strike aggressively in the direction of the form and clearly define it. The finished painting, while more suave, strikes an entirely different note.

MR. DAVID ROCKEFELLER (right)
Oil on canvas, 38 x 40" (97 x 102 cm), collection Pace University, New York. In painting a portrait, even if your distance from the sitter is only a few feet, you are dealing with aerial perspective. By exaggerating its effects and deliberately blurring such details as the base of the sculpture and the elbow and chair to our right, I achieve a sense of depth and focus attention on the figure. This is similar to "selective focus" in photography.

MR. COLIN PHIPPS *(left)*
Oil on canvas, 48 x 34" (122 x 86 cm), collection Mr. and Mrs. Colin Phipps. When Mr. Phipps posed for me in his Tallahassee home, he leaned against a small table stacked on top of another table, with a drapery covering both. I was able to turn this into fence rails without too much difficulty. The background cloud formations can be put in anywhere. To increase the outdoor effect (even though, of course, the figure was painted in the studio), I accentuated the downward light on the dark jacket, particularly in the sleeve to our left. Without the useful dark of the trees to soften the silhouette, the dark jacket would have been a problem against so light a background.

DETAIL OF THE HEAD *(above)*
Mr. Phipps is as handsome as a movie star. His face is accentuated by a secondary light source entering from our right, creating a cool side light. The highlight on the forehead is a mixture of white, alizarin crimson, and cadmium yellow light. The cool planes around the mouth have a touch of chromium oxide green in them. The white turtleneck shirt casts a cool reflected light under the chin.

MRS. COLIN PHIPPS (left)
Oil on canvas, 48 x 34" (122 x 86 cm), collection Mr. and Mrs. Phipps. Black passages, such as Mrs. Phipps' dress, do not have to be painted black but can be treated as a melange of rich colors. This reproduction does not show it fully, but in this black dress there are intense crimsons and purples throughout the darkest darks, and blues and greens in the lights. When painting cloud formations such as those in the background here, try for a pleasing arrangement. Place crisp edges here and there, and contrast them with soft edges, and contrast warm reflected lights with cool ones. Here it was important to keep even the lightest value in the clouds darker than the lightest accents in the hair so as to make the figure advance and background recede.

DETAIL OF THE HAIR (above)
Blond hair is beautiful to look at, but it can be extremely difficult to paint. The first lesson the closely observing painter learns is that the color is subdued and soft, not bright yellow as a beginning artist would paint it. It is basically a cool grayish mixture of soft, cool tones. Here, warm reflected light tones in the shadows help to enliven it.

MR. HERMANN HIRZEL
Oil on canvas, 36 x 28" (91 x 71 cm), collection Mr. and Mrs. Hirzel. The two paintings shown here were begun in the Hirzel's beautiful Zurich home and were designed as matching "pendant" portraits, so named because matching portrait miniatures were carried in a necklace pendant in medieval Europe. The conception of the portraits is deliberately formal and the large areas of open background are intended to balance each other. These open spaces are animated by the cast shadows and by a scumbling technique that introduced warm tones over cool ones and vice versa.

MRS. HERMANN HIRZEL

Oil on canvas, 36 x 28" (91 x 71 cm), collection Mr. and Mrs. Hirzel. A black dress adds a rich elegance to a portrait and is always exciting to paint. I softened the contours by merging the black dress with the dark of the shadows. Students sometimes ask for the "secret" of painting pearls, but there's no secret—just hard work. First the strands of pearls must be carefully drawn, then each pearl is painted separately. Each pearl has a light and a shadow area, a highlight, and a warm reflected light. Sargent was able to flick in a string of pearls with a single stroke each. That doesn't work for me, however. I have to patiently account for each pearl.

DR. JAMES FLETCHER

Oil on canvas, 48 x 34" (122 x 86 cm), collection National Aeronautics and Space Administration, Washington, D.C. NASA headquarters in Washington is alive with the romance and daring of the great space missions. Everything is high technology and futuristic. The sittings for this project were held in a conference room filled with every imaginable type of space-age communication apparatus. I tried to suggest some of this atmosphere with the deep, spacious sky and the small detail of the Atlas launcher. Dr. Fletcher has had a distinguished career in education and government service, and I tried to capture his great dignity, strength, and pervasive self-assurance.

DR. MILLICENT McINTOSH
Oil on canvas, 54 x 34" (137 x 86 cm), collection Barnard College, New York. The painting originally had an indoor setting, with a classical Greek column on the left and draperies filling most of the background. But after a number of sittings, the background seemed tight and stilted. One day I received a postcard from Dr. McIntosh, postponing the next sitting. When I turned the card over, I discovered a delightful Berkshire scene depicting the mountain near the subject's home. I joyfully removed the old background and copied the postcard scene you see here. I allowed the wind to ruffle the robe a bit, and the painting came alive.

Part IV

A Career in Portraiture

Portrait painting is an exciting profession with never a dull moment. Each assignment poses a new challenge, with fascinating, creative problems to solve.

Portrait painting is nondiscriminatory. Men and women of all ages have an equal opportunity in this field, and a college degree has no importance. Furthermore, there is no retirement age.

Through portraiture, you can meet some of the world's most interesting people. The sitters who come to my studio are usually big achievers in some way: university presidents, corporate executives, famous clergymen, scientists, and doctors—people who have made a big mark in life and are being honored with a portrait.

Portrait painting can be a very lucrative profession. Some of the famous portrait painters in history—Titian, Rubens, Gainsborough—lived like princes. Even today portrait painters are being paid handsomely for their work. The artists represented by Portraits, Incorporated, in New York, receive $2,000 to $30,000—and up—for each job. Your success as a portrait painter is not limited, but it does depend on your talent and drive.

Travel is an important part of this business. My work has taken me to London, Switzerland, Africa, and to most of the great cities of America in the past few years. The inconvenience of having to transport my equipment is more than compensated by the stimulation of a new environment.

I also want to say a good word for portraiture as a hobby. I greatly admire those who take up portrait painting as an avocational pursuit. Yes, it is the most difficult and demanding field of painting, but it is also a totally absorbing hobby.

Finally, the portraitist no longer needs an elegant studio in Manhattan. No matter where you live, there is a market for portraiture today.

8 Launching Your Career

Portrait painting is a difficult and demanding profession. The artists who succeed at it combine talent, determination, and hard work in an especially intense way.

Before you launch into this profession, analyze your motives, desires, and qualities. Here are some questions to ask yourself: Am I a "self-starter?" Am I intensely motivated to become a portrait painter? Do I want to do this more than anything in the world? Am I willing to work hard—really hard? Am I able to accept criticism, sorting out the just from the unjust criticism I am bound to receive, and am I mature enough to profit from it? Am I willing to make occasional compromises, as long as my artistic and personal integrity remains intact? And what about my self-image: Is it strong enough to survive the pushing and pulling that comes in the normal course of a career in the arts? If you can answer with a brave "yes" to these questions, let's push ahead.

Here are my recommendations for the steps to follow in making a start as a portrait painter.

1. Establish a Base of Operations. This is your studio. It should be simply a good workroom: clean, spacious, quiet, and with good north light. Make it a place that is conducive to work. Equip it and furnish it properly (see Chapters 1 and 2). Have your brushes and tools conveniently arranged and ready for use. Most of all, make it a private sanctuary where you alone are the master.

2. Prepare Some Good Samples. You should prepare at least three good samples, a man's portrait, a woman's portrait, and a child's portrait. The man's portrait should be 36 x 30" (91 x 76 cm), and the subject should be wearing a business suit. The portrait of a woman should also be 36 x 30", and she should be dressed somewhat on the formal side. The child's portrait should be 30 x 25" (76 x 64 cm) or 24 x 20" (61 x 51 cm). These portraits must be your very best work and should be painted just as if they were full-paying commissioned assignments. Frame them properly. Don't make the mistake of putting cheap frames on your samples, which can ruin the effect of your hard work.

3. Prepare an Attractive Portfolio of Your Work. This should be a looseleaf album containing color photographs of your samples and other completed portraits. The photographs should be 8 x 10" or 11 x 14" (20 x 25 or 28 x 35 cm). Don't begin the book with your best and most recent work and then go on to include everything you ever painted. The portfolio should include *only* your best work. Be selective and reject the prints of work you have outgrown and gone beyond. It is better to show a small sampling of top-notch work than to include reams of mediocre work. And most important, *do not include any student work*—no pastel nudes from the life class. Figure 40 shows an example of the type of portfolio I describe.

4. *Prepare a Piece of Printed Promotion.* This should be a well-designed pamphlet or brochure that includes reproductions of your best work. Again, be selective and include only the best. There are many, many forms this promotional piece can take, and you may want to enlist the help of someone in the commercial art field to help you design your brochure. My brochure has an 8½ x 11″ (21 x 28 cm) format of eight pages and is printed in black and white. This is, of course, standard business-letter size and is ideal for filing. You cannot sell someone a portrait unless it is already wanted, but if you make your promotion piece attractive, people may save it and you may hear from your prospect at a much later time. Be sure to include your address and phone number. Your price list should be printed on a separate sheet and may or may not be included, since it is often best to locate an interested client first and talk prices later. Do have your prices set and in print, however, so there is no question later regarding the cost of your work.

5. *Have a Business Card and a Business Letterhead Printed.* A professional artist should be as prepared with proper business materials as any other professional. My personal preference is for a simple engraved card and letterhead that could just as easily be used by a doctor or an attorney.

6. *Work to Establish Yourself with a Gallery and/or an Agent.* It is never easy for an artist to sell his own work. We artists tend to be rather shy and

40. THE PORTFOLIO
A presentation book with copies of your work is a "must" for the professional portrait artist. My book is a black looseleaf binder with clear vinyl leaves that accept 14 x 17″ (35 x 43 cm) sheets. The sheets are gray "cover stock" with 11 x 14″ (28 x 35 cm) professionally taken color prints, mounted and bordered. On the opposite page is the subject's name and title.

PAINTING FOR A TIMELESS PLACE
Oil on canvas, for a condensation of the book by Ellen Bromfield Geld, courtesy The Reader's Digest. *There are many opportunities for the portrait painter in the field of publishing. This painting was used as the title-page decoration of a book, but it essentially is a group portrait, and I approached it the same way I would a regular commission. I used professional New York models as my subjects and painted it in oil on canvas.*

are usually modest about our work. If you can find someone who likes your work very much and believes in you as an artist, suggest that he or she consider becoming your agent. An enthusiastic agent is a wonderful asset. Equip your agent with proper materials to sell your work—your brochure, your portfolio, and your price list.

Be anxious to pay your agent his share of the determined fee. My gallery in New York earns 40% of the price of the painting, and I don't begrudge them one nickel of it. They earn it, many times over! They provide gallery space that is always available to the public. They work out the details of the cost of the painting and only contact me when a job is set. An added advantage of the gallery is that the client can compare my work with other artists' work and be rather sure he will get what he wants. In other words, he has selected *my* style from among other styles. Try taking your samples to an established gallery in your area and offer them a commission on your fee. The gallery will be helpful in determining a price schedule that is realistic for your work. Some galleries ask for as much as 50% of the fee, but if they produce work for you, it may well be worth it to become "partners" with them.

PAINTING FOR A TIMELESS PLACE
Oil on canvas, courtesy **The Reader's Digest.** *This painting is another example of how portraiture can be used in publications. Neighborhood children and a fascinating character from the sidewalks of the Bowery were my subjects here.*

9

The Business Side of Portraiture

Make up your mind right from the beginning to be businesslike—to be a solid professional. Integrity, reliability, honesty, fairness, attention to detail, perseverance—these are the qualities that succeed here, as in any endeavor.

To be a good business person, you need a business office. This may be a corner of the studio where you have your desk, typewriter, filing cabinet, and telephone, preferably equipped with an automatic answering device (Figure 41).

RECORD KEEPING

A thorough and efficient record-keeping system is basic to any business. This may involve considerable work, but it's absolutely necessary. To make matters easier for you, I recommend the following system, which involves three drawers in a standard filing cabinet:

Drawer One: Financial Records. Check and cash payment receipts (art supplies, books, permanent equipment, dues and fees, electricity, maintenance and repair, office supplies, petty cash, photography expenses, photostats, postage, printing, rent receipts, shipping costs, telephone, typesetting, travel and entertainment).

Miscellaneous records (advertising, checkbook statements, income tax records, insurance, lease, occupancy tax records, salaries, sales-tax records).

Drawer Two: Portrait Job Records/Idea File. Portrait job records (current commissions, past commissions, advertising and promotion, biography and personal photos, framing records, model records, price policy).

Ideal File (men's portraits, women's portraits, children's portraits, group portraits, backgrounds, other artists' work).

Drawer Three: Photography. Contact sheets (a good numbering system for negatives is one using the year, month, day, and roll number—for example, 800625-1 would mean June 25, 1980, Roll 1), negatives, copies of completed work, reference photographs.

If you equip your filing cabinet with a folder for each of the categories listed and arrange them in three drawers as suggested, you'll have half the battle won.

INCOME TAX RETURNS

Here is a list of categories used in preparing Schedule C, *Profit or Loss from Business or Profession*. Many of these categories coincide with my filing categories described under "Record Keeping," or are a combination of information that must be assembled at tax time.

Advertising. Includes costs of typesetting, printing of brochures, etc.

Art Supplies.

Bank Charges. If you use your checking account as your business account, bank charges are deductible.

Books.

Depreciation. A percentage of the cost of new equipment with a life longer than a year is deductible. Keep all receipts. Don't forget to take a tax credit for investment in new equipment.

Dues and Fees. Art clubs, societies, legal fees, accountant's fee, etc.

Electricity.

Interest on Business Loans.

Maintenance of Rental Property. Or portion of home used as studio and business area. Includes costs of hardware, lumber, paint, etc.

Miscellaneous. Should be a relatively small amount.

Model Fees.

Moving Expenses. Properly apportioned.

Office Supplies.

Photography and Photo Supplies.

Postage.

Rent. Or properly apportioned percentage of home costs.

Telephone.

Travel and Entertainment. Keep ledgers and receipts while traveling on business.

42. COMMISSION DETAILS FORM (opposite page) I composed and printed up this form to record and keep track of my various assignments.

PRICING YOUR WORK

Most galleries and agents work out a schedule of prices for each artist based on the size of the painting and increasing in reasonably logical increments. The price for the 36 x 30" size is the basic price and the one you should set with the most care. Here's some good advice. After having talked with hundreds of artists from all over the country at our annual seminar in New York, I am convinced that most portrait artists tend to undervalue their work. Don't make this mistake, even when you are just beginning your career. In short, price your work at the highest level you can command. Explore the market and try to learn what prices are being paid for work similar to yours. As your work improves and your reputation grows, raise your prices periodically to reflect this. My own experience has been very reassuring: each time I have increased my prices, I have found that I have more work coming in. I have found myself dealing with the top echelons of the business and professional world, and it has been a great privilege over the years to get to know as my sitters so many distinguished men and women. My clients are distinguished professional people, and they expect me to be professional about my work.

Most price schedules are worked out on the basis of several standard sizes. They also vary with the artist's ability, experience, and reputation. The following table ("Suggested Price Schedules") contains seven graduated price levels. Again, these are only *suggested* price ranges, to show you how prices can vary within each level of ability and experience. The actual prices are only arbitrary. You can, of course, set any price you wish on your work. (Remember also that these prices reflect 1981 standards.)

SUGGESTED PRICE SCHEDULES

24 x 20″ Head and shoulders	$50	$125	$250	$500	$1,000	$1,500	
30 x 25″ Larger head and shoulders. May include hands	100	250	500	1,000	2,000	3,000	5,000
36 x 30″ Basic ¾ length	150	375	750	1,500	3,000	4,500	7,500
40 x 32″ Larger ¾ length	200	500	1,000	2,000	4,000	6,000	10,000
Full length	300	750	1,500	3,000	6,000	9,000	15,000

In New York both 30 x 24″ (76 x 61 cm) and 30 x 25″ (76 x 64 cm) are considered standard sizes, perhaps because Portraits, Incorporated—the largest portrait gallery in the world—often writes commissions for 30 x 25″.

Once the price of a commission is set, I never refer to it again. I concentrate on doing the best painting I possibly can to suit the job. If a 30 x 24″ painting has been commissioned but I feel that the composition calls for a much larger portrait, I never hesitate to paint the larger canvas for the agreed-on price. It's important to remember, especially when you're establishing your career, that a painting will stand forever as an example of your work and that few people, if any, will ever know what you were paid for it. So always do the best job you can, and I guarantee that your prices won't stay on any one level for very long. They will go up!

PAYMENT
I don't collect the fee for my work until the painting is finished, delivered, approved, and hung, and after the gallery has sent a bill and received payment. This can sometimes be a remarkably long period, although I have never *not* received payment. I do know that some artists insist on a one-third deposit and full payment on delivery. However, the idea of a deposit

can lead an artist to become overly cautious with his work and produce a tight, lifeless portrait. Don't let prices and money lead you to compromise your style.

I feel that financial arrangements should be kept in the background as much as possible, and since I do most of my work through my New York gallery, my involvement in this aspect is minimal. A good agent or gallery will set the best price possible for you, will handle packing and delivery, and will send out invoices. If the commission comes outside a gallery, it may be a good idea to receive a deposit before beginning. I have mixed feelings on this subject, since without the deposit, as my friend and colleague Robert Bruce Williams puts it, you have the *freedom to fail*, which may help keep your painting from becoming overly worked and tightly finished. A good gallery or agent is invaluable, and I go out of my way to send my gallery its commission, even on second- and third-generation paintings if the source for someone's interest in my work is a painting I did for my gallery.

10 Conclusion

There is no standing still as a portrait artist. You must continue to study and grow throughout your career. Your motto should be "Never anything but my best!" and you should strive to make each painting better than the one that preceded it.

THE TEN KEYS TO SUCCESS

As your career unfolds, there are ten attitudes that I feel you must cultivate to promote your personal growth and unlock the door to success.

1. *Enthusiasm.* This is the master key to success as an artist. The successful artist gets genuinely excited about his work. He makes every painting the very best painting of which he is capable, regardless of the time, effort, and expense involved. His motto is "Never anything but my best, whatever the cost."

2. *Self-discipline—The Capacity for Hard Work.* Every successful artist is a hard worker. He is not afraid of long hours because he knows that there is no substitute for hard work. As the saying goes, painting—good painting—is 10% inspiration and 90% perspiration. Sargent would repaint his portraits repeatedly until he was satisfied or until he felt he had done his absolute best.

3. *Definite Purpose.* This is the starting point of all great achievement. One's goals in life should be specific; in fact, they should be *in writing* and read often—even daily. The artist must decide what kind of painter he wants to be. He must narrow his heroes to one or two and then study their work and emulate them. He collects examples of work that he intends to equal, and then surpass.

4. *An Honest Vision.* A great painter has an intense desire to get at the truth of a subject. He sees objectively, and his painting reflects the integrity of an honest vision. Nothing is improvised or imagined. Everything is based on actual observation. He indulges in no flattery in his portraiture, no fakery in his backgrounds—only honest, fair reporting.

5. *A Capacity for Self-criticism.* Every real artist is hungry for criticism and invites it from every side. Norman Rockwell would ask every person who came into his studio what he thought of the picture on the easel. Even the boy delivering groceries was invited to comment. But beyond this, you must develop the art of self-criticism, of being able to judge your own paintings candidly. You must be ruthless in criticizing your own work. In fact, your criticism must be more intense than the criticism of friends and teachers.

6. *Learning to Be Yourself.* Paint a subject the way *you* see it. Paint to satisfy yourself. When you have painted a portrait that thrills *you*, it will certainly please the client, too. Develop a strong self-image. The real artist is hungry for criticism, but he also knows in the final analysis that the painting must satisfy the painter above all else.

7. *Going the Extra Mile.* Remember the motto: "Never anything but your best, whatever the cost." Always do your best work, regardless of the time, effort, and expense involved. When you have been commissioned to paint a head-and-shoulders portrait, but a three-quarter-length one is necessary to tell the full story of your subject, *paint it* and deliver it for the same price as the head and shoulders. If the painting is not a total and unqualified success, paint a second version, and a third, until you—and the client—are satisfied. Make sketches, studies, and other preliminary work, whatever is required to arrive at the very best solution. This is going the extra mile in portraiture.

8. *Always Be a Student.* Every successful artist has an eternal curiosity about his craft and art, the desire to discover a better way. This impels him to join painting classes or attend seminars to exchange "shop talk." The true artist wants to stay fresh, to renew himself, to "stay out of ruts." Complacency is deadly to an artist. A vague feeling of dissatisfaction with your progress is healthy and leads to paths of renewal.

9. *Absolute Integrity in Business Dealings.* The successful portrait artist is proud of his profession and is conscious of its great heritage. You should pledge yourself to maintain the dignity of your profession. You should conduct and conclude all financial transactions with courtesy and discretion, being fair, honest, and straightforward.

10. *Perseverance.* Don't be discouraged. It is only natural that some of your paintings will be better than others, but try to keep your average up. Continue to work hard. If you have a setback, pick yourself up and push ahead. Never look back. When they asked Picasso which of his hundreds of paintings was his favorite, he replied, "The next one." Your masterpiece, your *Mona Lisa,* may be the next picture that you do.

I have tried to sum up the qualities of a portrait artist in the following pledge I composed for the Portrait Club of New York, now the Portrait Institute:

THE PORTRAIT ARTIST'S PLEDGE

As a portrait artist, I am proud of my profession and conscious of its great heritage. I pledge myself to the maintaining of the dignity of my profession. I pledge that every painting that leaves my studio will represent my very finest effort as a creative artist and a craftsman. The painting I am working on *now* is the most important one of all to me, and I will spare no effort to make it the finest work of art of which I am capable. I pledge that I will employ only fine-quality materials and will take the traditional precautions to ensure the permanence of my creations. I am conscious that I am producing not only a portrait but also an enduring work of art.

DR. TORREY WITH O.E. SANDEN
Courtesy **Decision** *Magazine. This painting was commissioned by The Billy Graham Association to illustrate a story about my late father (a Presbyterian clergyman) and his encounter with the famous evangelist, Dr. Reuben A. Torrey. I used a professional model for the figure of Dr. Torrey and posed myself for my father's profile.*

Suggested Reading

Balcomb, Mary N. *Nicolai Fechin.* USA: Northland Press, 1975.

Bates, Kenneth. *Brackman, His Art and Teaching.* Conn., Madison Art Gallery Publishing Company, 1973.

Blake, Wendon. *Creative Color: A Practical Guide for Oil Painters.* New York: Watson-Guptill, and London: Pitman Publishing, 1972.

Burns, Paul C., and Joe Singer. *The Portrait Painter's Problem Book.* New York: Watson-Guptill Publications, 1979.

Charteris, Evan. *John Sargent.* New York: Charles Scribner's Sons, 1927.

Coke, Van Deren. *The Painter and the Photograph.* New Mexico: University of New Mexico Press, 1964.

Doerner, Max. *The Materials of the Artist: And Their Use in Painting with Notes on the Techniques of the Old Masters.* New York: Harcourt Brace Jovanovich, 1949.

Eastman Kodak Company. *Professional Portrait Techniques.* Rochester, N.Y., 1973.

Greene, Daniel. *Pastel: A Comprehensive Guide to Pastel Painting.* New York: Watson-Guptill, and London: Pitman Publishing, 1974.

Guptill, Arthur. *Norman Rockwell Illustrator.* New York: Watson-Guptill, 1946.

Henri, Robert. *The Art Spirit.* New York: J. B. Lippincott, 1930.

Hogarth, Burne. *Drawing the Human Head.* New York: Watson-Guptill, 1967.

Kelley, Ramon, and Mary Carroll Nelson. *Ramon Kelley Paints Portraits and Figures.* New York: Watson-Guptill, and London: Pitman Publishing, 1977.

Kinstler, Everett Raymond. *Painting Portraits.* New York: Watson-Guptill, 1971.

Loomis, Andrew. *Creative Illustration.* New York: The Viking Press, 1947.

———. *Three-Dimensional Drawing.* New York: The Viking Press, 1961.

———. *Figure Drawing for All It's Worth.* New York: The Viking Press, 1964.

———. *Drawing the Head and Hands.* New York: The Viking Press, 1970.

Mann, Harrington. *The Techniques of Portrait Painting.* Philadelphia: J. B. Lippincott Company.

Mayer, Ralph. *The Artist's Handbook.* New York: The Viking Press, 1964.

Nibbelink, Don D. *Picturing People.* Garden City, N.Y.: American Photographic Book Publishing Company, 1976.

Ormond, Richard. *John Singer Sargent: Paintings, Drawings, Watercolors.* New York: Harper & Row, 1970.

Sanden, John Howard. *Painting the Head in Oil.* Edited by Joe Singer. New York: Watson-Guptill, and London: Pitman Publishing, 1976.

Scharf, Aaron. *Art and Photography.* Baltimore, Md.: Penguin Books, 1968.

Schmid, Richard. *Richard Schmid Paints the Figure.* New York: Watson-Guptill, and London: Pitman Publishing, 1973.

Silverman, Burt. *Painting People.* New York: Watson-Guptill, and London: Pitman Publishing, 1977.

Singer, Joe. *Painting Men's Portraits.* New York: Watson-Guptill, and London, Pitman Publishing, 1977.

———. *Painting Women's Portraits.* New York: Watson-Guptill, and London, Pitman Publishing, 1977.

———. *How to Paint Portraits In Pastel.* New York: Watson-Guptill, and London, Pitman Publishing, 1972.

Index

(Note: Page numbers in italics refer to paintings or illustrations.)